STREAMLI

MW01698627

At Your FINGERTIPS in the Office

The filing system described in this book is a suggested model only. The information provided herein is given with the understanding that the authors are not providing legal, accounting or other professional advice. For specific advice regarding your business records, please consult your legal advisor, accountant or financial manager.

STREAMLINE AND ORGANIZE

At Your FINGERTIPS in the Office

Information Management for the Small Business

Alexandra Bradley and Denise Dale

For small-business owners everywhere. May you always have the information you need right at your fingertips.

00 01 02 03 04 5 4 3 2 1

Streamline Information and Organizing Services
186-8120 No. 2 Rd, Ste #271
Richmond, British Columbia
V7C 5J8
www.streamlinebooks.com

Also available: *At Your Fingertips! A Household Filing System That Works for You.* ISBN 0-9685727-0-7

Canadian Cataloguing in Publication Data
Bradley, Alexandra E., 1948–
At your fingertips in the office

Includes bibliographical references and index.

ISBN 0-9685727-1-5

1. Small business—Records and correspondence—Management. I. Dale, Denise, 1961– II. Title.
HF5736.B72 2000 651.5 C00-910881-5

Editing: Paper Trail Publishing
Design: Carty Design
Distributed by Raincoast Book*Express*

Printed in Canada by Friesens

Contents

Introduction

INFORMATION MANAGEMENT IS ONE OF THE MAJOR HEADACHES for small-business owners. This is especially true for home-based business owners, whose business papers get mixed up with household information and whose space is limited. What to keep? Where to put it? For how long? Why? Are paper or computer records best? Where do you start, and why is it so important to get paperwork and information under control? What benefits will you reap from getting organized? We tackled similar dilemmas in our book on household records management, *At Your Fingertips! A Household Filing System That Works for You.* Information management for a small business, home-based or not, is more complex. Beyond the filing and retrieval aspects, there are regulations and external requirements. But the benefits of appropriate information management remain the same.

Save Time

The major reason for organizing paperwork is that it will save time—precious time that you, as a small-business owner, do not have. Misplaced information costs both time and money and adds to your stress level. Consider the following scenarios:

- The deadline for filing tax is tomorrow, and you can't find some of the telephone statements that you need.

You spend the morning tearing the office apart and do a thorough search of any other likely spots, including your kitchen and your car—your mobile office. You call the telephone company, which can provide the statements (for a charge, of course), and you brave rush-hour traffic to collect the copies because it's too late for a courier to pick them up. Whew! You arrive home lighter in the wallet, with more miles on your aging car, behind schedule, with a headache, and having lost a day's time.

- A client telephones to discuss the details of your current project, and you cannot quickly obtain the file with the relevant data in it.
- You find yourself creating a new invoice form each billing period because you can't find the standard form you have already created and filed . . . somewhere.

The list of such situations is endless, and given a moment, you can probably think of several of your own where mismanagement of information has caused you grief. You are not alone—information management is an administrative dilemma faced by business owners large and small.

Save Money

In large organizations there is usually a person or department responsible for controlling and filing information. There are written guidelines and procedures telling workers where to keep information, for how long, why and in what formats. These organizations are aware of the cost of lost documents and inefficient information management practices. Small-business owners, however, are on their own. They must create routines and procedures from scratch, along with all the other aspects of running a business. This book takes the guesswork out of managing information and saves you from having to reinvent the wheel.

A survey of available studies and literature has shown that workers in knowledge-based organizations can spend as much as 20 percent of their time (one working day per week) looking for, or waiting for, "lost" information. Sources in records management peg the cost of a lost or misfiled document between $80 and $150 US. What is the real cost to your business? It is virtually impossible to calculate if you take into account the ramifications beyond the filing-and-finding aspects, for example, the time taken to re-create lost paperwork, delayed decisions, unhappy customers or a lost contract.

Save Space

Keeping too much information, because you don't have time to deal with it or you think you might need it someday, costs you in terms of space, equipment and supplies. Whatever you keep should be relevant, retrievable and worthy of retention. No matter what you keep, you should know where it is and, in most cases, be able to get it within moments.

Protect Your Business

Your business records document your actions, and a key consideration must be to save the records that protect your business. The information in records must be available to support your decisions. This future reference may be for evidence of your decisions in litigation or to produce records in compliance with legal or regulatory requirements. Most important, to plan your future actions, you need to refer to your past activities. As time passes, the day-to-day operating value of your records will be surpassed by the secondary or research value that the records can provide for your future needs. (This may be difficult to keep in mind when you are focusing on the immediate needs of your business!)

This book helps you decide what information to keep. It helps you determine where to put it and for how long. The book includes a model filing system that you can adopt as is or modify to suit your business needs. No book on information management would be complete without a discussion of electronic records, including electronic mail and the impact of the Internet on records. Information about protecting records and their content is also included. You will also find some practical tips, advice, hands-on instructions and a list of resources, including websites, to round out the information you may need to set up and maintain your information management system.

Don't delegate information management to someone else in your organization, no matter how tempting this may be. At least not in the beginning. As the owner-operator, you are the person most aware of the value of your records to the present and future operation of your business. So, just as in big organizations, you must set some realistic policies based on your needs. Once you have worked out the requirements and processes, then, by all means, involve others and train everyone to follow the systems we are going to help you set up. But if you yourself are not aware from the outset of every aspect of your business, you might lose valuable information.

For those of you who think that the solution to the paperwork management dilemma is to throw a computer at it, we say "Don't you believe it!" Paperwork is alive and well, and in our computer age it is proliferating at a more rapid rate than ever. Computers are useful tools that can help with record keeping, but they don't resolve the basic issues. In fact, without a coherent strategy for information management, introducing computers will only create another level of complexity and yet more dilemmas for you. You'll find more on using computers in information management in chapter 4.

The purpose of this book is to provide you with an organizing strategy that will simplify the flow of information through your company so you can focus your energy on the development of your business. Sound simple? You bet! We give you the principles and help you set up the procedures that will streamline and effectively manage the information you need to succeed.

1
What to Keep?
Making Decisions

ONE QUESTION THAT ALWAYS STUMPS PEOPLE WHO ARE RUNNING small businesses is "What to keep?" Why is this such a hard question? Usually the business owner knows that *some* records are keepers, but often isn't sure exactly which of all the incoming or outgoing records will have later value. And who has time to think about it? It's usually easier to keep *everything* and put it aside to review later. Then, when "later" never comes, the pile gets put into a box out of sight. Before you know it, the boxes have hatched into a whole nested nightmare of unsorted paper chaos, a mixture of needed and unneeded items.

What are your record-keeping habits? Are you a keeper or a tosser? There are two extreme types of paperwork managers: the keepers, who will keep everything "just in case," and the tossers, who, in the name of efficiency, will throw out everything to "control the clutter." Most of us fall somewhere in between—we keep some things, toss others. But we don't have a rationale, and when the time comes to find documents, we can't tell if we've thrown something out or kept it. Be aware that each extreme has its problems, and being in between is no help either. The key is to have a rationale based on the business's needs and obligations.

Whatever you do keep should be maintained in an organized system, whether the information is on paper or in an electronic format. The name of the game is retrieval—

can you find the information when you need it?

There are rules that affect some types of business records. Particularly, there are government rules and regulations that dictate how long to keep records and where records must be kept. Your business may also be affected by rules that dictate what information you may or may not collect, such as other people's personal data.

Whether such regulations apply to you depends on the nature of your business. Think about what your business does and do some checking to find out if your business is affected by specific rules. Ask your legal and financial advisors. Many business owners, particularly when starting out, find that they need comply only with taxation rules. We will examine the reasons for keeping information, including "the rules," in more detail in chapter 3.

Most businesses of any size or nature have two types of records: records associated with the administration of the business *(administrative records)*, and records that fulfill the purpose of the business *(operational records)*.

Administrative records usually are information on financials (accounts payable and receivable), equipment, office premises or facilities, and employees. No matter what kind of business, it will usually have administrative records for some of these areas.

Operational records include records directly associated with what the business does, such as project files, sales files and customer files. These types of records can be very different from one business to another, even when the businesses do the same type of work.

Depending on the type of business you run and where you are located, a selection of each type of record may be required by outside agencies, such as taxation authorities, to be kept for a specified period of time. You will also want to keep records for your own reference, to help you plan, evaluate and develop your business. As your business develops, you will want to keep a company history or archival record. (Who knows, should you become world-famous, these records would have social relevance and value!)

If you can decide the value of the information you receive before you have too much of it, you can simplify the decisions about what records to keep and for how long. And you will know why you are keeping these records—and why you are throwing others out.

The value of records can be determined by asking yourself the following questions:

- *Does this record have administrative value?* Does this information help me to administer my business, for example, to keep track of major decisions (as would minutes of meetings), identify equipment warranties or prove I hold insurance?
- *Does this record have financial value?* Does this information help me determine who owes me money or to whom I owe money? Is it something that I will require for taxation or audit reasons?
- *Does this record have operational value?* Does this information help me to operate my business, for example, to keep in touch with customers, identify my process for manufacturing or document my course outline and teaching notes for my training program?
- *Does this record have legal or regulatory value?* Does this information help me to keep track of my business rights or obligations, as would a business licence, a property lease, incorporation documents or name registration papers?

- *Does this record have reference value?* Is this information of interest to me, or for me to refer to, but not directly related to the running of my business? Examples might include magazines, product catalogues, newsletters, news clippings, conference proceedings and publications.
- *Does this record have historic or archival value?* Will this information be of interest to me or others in the future, to tell the story of the company or business? Such information could include company press releases, company publications or newsletters, photographs of special events, and information about products and services.

Another factor to consider in making decisions about what to keep and for how long is the *life cycle of records*. Just like people, information has a life cycle. Information is received, and records are created and used to make decisions. They are filed for retrieval, then stored for a further period of time. Ultimately, few records are kept permanently. In most organizations, about 95 percent of all records are destroyed. In large organizations, the life cycle of information is usually the basis for all records management planning. Some kind of records retention schedule is usually used as a blueprint for instructing employees which records are to be kept and for how long.

What is the life cycle of business information? In most businesses, information that has been recently created or received is the information needed close at hand to make appointments, do work, sell products, contact customers. This is the *active phase* of the life cycle. Even after the information is acted on, it will still need to be referred to.

After time passes, the need to refer to information

drops off. Information then moves from the active phase to the *inactive (or semi-active) phase*. During this period, the records may not need to be referred to, but may need to be kept to fulfill regulatory obligations or for historic reference. When it is no longer necessary to keep records for legal or regulatory reasons, records pass into the *final disposition phase* of their life cycle, in which records are kept permanently or disposed of. Information that has historic or archival value is treated as permanent records, which are retained indefinitely, in safekeeping.

These principles of records management and the life cycle of records (discussed in more detail in chapter 3) apply equally well to the information generated by large and small businesses. With an understanding of your business values and requirements, applying them to a small or home-based business can ensure that unnecessary records do not accumulate and become a burden for the already busy entrepreneur.

Tip: Know What You Have

Grab a notepad and conduct a quick written survey of your existing records to discover what kinds of information you have, in what formats and where they are located. Don't get bogged down with detailed notes. This survey is just an overview to help you understand the nature and content of your records.

A comprehensive survey of your records may be necessary if you're working to organize a large collection of records. The survey form included here provides you with a framework for the types of questions you might ask about your records.

Records Survey

Date:

Completed by:

Records Series Title:

Department or Work Group Name (if applicable):

Description (types of documents, how arranged):

Date Range (from year/month to year/month):

Volume (how many inches of files):

Format (non-paper):

Retention Period (if known):

Type of Storage Equipment (type of cabinet or storage method):

Use of Security Devices (locks, passwords, restricted access):

Location (office, storage room, off-site location name):

Uses of Information:

Who uses these records?

How often are records referenced?

Is information confidential?

Is this a vital records series? (What would happen if this information were lost?)

Remember that the function of this exercise is to provide you with enough information to set up the records control procedures we discuss in the next chapters. If you don't know some of the answers, such as the retention period, don't worry, you can always come back later and fill in the details after reading the rest of the book.

To summarize, you begin to develop an information management strategy by finding out the obligations and requirements of records for your business operations. The next step toward solving the organizing dilemma is deciding what has value to your business: what should you be keeping? When you keep only the necessary records, you simplify the flow of information through your business. This in turn will simplify your daily operations, clear the paper clutter, streamline electronic records and ensure that you have the information you need for whatever requirements may arise. Now you need to determine where to put the information so you can find it when you need it.

2
Where to Put It?

Getting Organized

ONCE YOU HAVE DECIDED WHAT TO KEEP, THE NEXT STEP IS TO determine where to put your records so you can find them again. By where to put them, we mean two distinct concepts: first, the logical system for organizing the records (discussed in this chapter), and second, the right kind of physical home—equipment, folders, labelling and other maintenance matters (covered in chapter 5).

Let's discuss a logical arrangement for your records. Records in any form—paper, electronic, photographic, publications—are best kept in organized filing systems and in appropriate locations for quick access. A logical arrangement is based on function or topic, grouping information into familiar and meaningful categories. The goal is for you or any of your employees to be able to follow the logic of the arrangement to find any single item quickly and easily, whether it be a piece of paper or an electronic file.

Even when there is only one person—you—looking for information, a logical system helps you remember more easily where you put information and gives you a quick trail back to where you put your papers. When there are more people involved in the business, the logical and systematic approach is even more important, since no two people place papers in the same location unless they follow the same logic. What we're talking about here is similar to a system of traffic control. Rules are established that everyone can follow, and traffic should flow quickly and without accidents.

The business filing system described in this book divides information into four broad categories, based on its frequency of reference or use in the office:

Fingertip Files
Business Files
Permanent Files
Reference Files

These categories help you decide where to put records so that you can find them when you need them. They will also help you determine how long to keep information, a topic discussed further in chapter 3.

Fingertip Files

This information is time-sensitive and needs to be somewhere in the office where you or your staff can get at it quickly. In large organizations, this type of material is sometimes called the action file, tickler file or abeyance file, because it needs to be available for quick reference or is needed on a particular date. Also, information in this category is usually to be acted upon quickly, then transferred, if necessary, to the Business, Permanent or Reference Files.

How to Organize Fingertip Files

Start by subdividing time-sensitive information into three broad categories, which you can expand or condense to suit your business needs. These are:

Calendar
Contacts/Organizations
Receipts

The *Calendar* category is a system based on calendar dates to keep track of appointments, commitments and things to do. It allows you to file date-sensitive information and papers by date for retrieval as they are needed. In a one-person office, personal schedules can also be included here. Otherwise, it is best to keep only business-related information in the *Calendar.* Here is a place to file, for example, a note to send back a proposal response on April 16. Other examples include:

Appointments
Bills to Pay
Bring-Forward Information (for action on specific dates)
Callback Information
Special Event Notices
Tickets (travel, events)
To-Do Lists
Travel Arrangements

The *Contacts/Organizations* category includes business cards and other contact information you need to keep track of addresses, organizations, clients, service people and so on. You may have an electronic system for tracking some of this data, but a place to put the hard-copy items is also helpful. If you have several staff members, a central file such as this will enable everyone in the office to coordinate their activities and find what they need in one spot. A caution, though, about contact information: if it is outdated, you may be operating under incorrect assumptions and wasting time or resources. Examples of information to file here include:

Business Cards
Client Contact Information
Newsletters
Schedules (of outside organizations, transportation timetables—bus, train, ferry)

The *Receipts* category is a temporary holding place for receipts until they can be verified and matched to account statements or invoices. No more throwing the contents of your wallet into a shoebox! Your accountant will love you for this, and you will save money by reducing the amount of time you spend searching for stray pieces of paper. (Receipts in this category are the acknowledgements, verifications and slips that you or your employees receive as you conduct transactions on behalf of your business. Receipts that you issue to customers are not kept here. They will be part of your sales records and are discussed under Business Files.) Examples of papers to file here include:

Automobile/Transportation Receipts (cabs, rentals, bus fare)
Bank Machine/ATM Transaction Receipts
Cash Transaction Receipts
Courier and Shipping Receipts
Credit Card Receipts
Parking Receipts
Petty Cash Receipts
Project/Expense-Related Receipts

Any of these categories in the Fingertip Files can be

expanded if need be. For example, if you have several people working in your office, you might create a category for each person, or you might expand specific categories for individual employees. *Receipts* can be set up to read "Parking Receipts—Jane Brown"; "Parking Receipts—John Smith." If your company has several offices, you can establish these categories and subdivide them by office location, for example, Fingertip Files—Richmond; Fingertip Files—West Vancouver.

Fingertip Files should be kept in a centrally located place, where they can be readily reached while you are on the phone or heading out the door to a meeting. Usage determines where you put things, and the information in the Fingertip Files will be needed promptly and should be right at your fingertips. Keep it close at hand, and let everyone in the office know where it is.

Tip: Make Your Fingertip Files Portable

Make your Fingertip Files convenient to carry by keeping them in a binder. Then you can quickly grab the binder as you dash out the door, confident that all the information you need to conduct business while on the go is truly at your fingertips. See Appendix A for hands-on instructions.

Business Files

These records are the heart of your business. They relate to the running of your business, beyond the immediate actions located in the Fingertip Files. In a typical business, most of the records will reside here for a time. In fact, this information can travel—you may move information from the Fingertip Files after you have acted on it (for example, paid a bill) to a logical place within the Business Files where you can find the information when you need it. Much of the information in the Business Files is required for a particular period of time, after which it is moved again—in some cases to the shredder and then out the door. In other cases, it is moved into the Permanent Files.

How to Organize Business Files

In the Business Files you will want to set up categories that relate to your business needs or functions. Arrangement by subject or topic is usually the easiest to remember. Here you will need a filing system that is simple to set up and operate and, more importantly, will help you find information quickly when you need it later. Remember we mentioned that there are two kinds of business records—*administrative records* (housekeeping files common to most businesses) and *operational records* (unique information related to your specific business).

Administrative Files

Here are some typical examples of administrative records. Note that many of these categories may have expenses, but you will want to keep all financial information, including expenses and receipts, within the *Finance* category to enable you or your accountant to track costs.

Administration (or Office Administration)

- Insurance
- Legal Matters
- Meetings
- Memberships
- Publicity/Public Relations
- Travel (arrangements, reservations, but not expenses)

Equipment, Supplies and Services

- Catalogues, Manuals, Price Lists
- Computers—Hardware
- Computers—Software
- Computers—Network
- Furniture and Equipment
- Postal, Courier and Freight
- Stationery
- Vehicle(s)

Finance

- Accounting System and Procedures
- Accounts Payable
- Accounts Receivable
- Banking
- Credit Cards
- Expenses (travel, car)
- Financial Statements
- Salaries and Wages
- Suppliers (correspondence, excluding payable information)
- Taxation

Personnel and Staffing

- General Personnel Matters
- Benefits
- Contractors and Subcontractors
- Employees
- Health and Safety (workers' compensation)
- Hiring and Recruitment
- Training

Premises

- Lease
- Maintenance (cleaning, repairs)
- Utilities (heat, light, telecommunications)

Operational Files

Unlike the administrative files, which are fairly standard for most businesses, operational files are unique and related to your specific business. For example, if your business is a consulting practice, your operational files will consist of client and/or project files. If you are a sales organization, you will have client files but you will also have product and inventory files. A craft business would have supply files, product files and wholesale/retail customer files. Freelance writers, like consultants, will have project files. Obviously the list goes on, but as you can see, the types of files are similar but specific to the nature of each business. Examples include:

Business Plan (financial, operational)
Customers/Clients
Inventory (raw materials, finished products)
Marketing
Presentations and Seminars (that you or your company give)
Product Sales
Projects
Supplies

Each of these categories can certainly be further expanded or subdivided depending on the size of your business. For example, if you have more than one customer, you will have individual files by customer name under "Customers/Clients." If you sell products and have more than one product for sale, you can subdivide your "Product Sales" category by product, distributor, region or any other meaningful category that suits your sales functions. In contrast to "Product Sales," in the "Marketing" category, keep information about your various marketing, advertising and publicity activities.

Once you have established your Business Files categories, write a list of your broad file categories and your individual file titles. This file list should be placed at the front of your filing cabinet. It is your key reference document or index for later finding the information. You may choose to create a computer database as a finding aid. Depending upon how many files you have, you might want to consider assigning a numeric or alphanumeric code to the files. We'll talk more about coding, labelling and filing the items in chapter 5.

The Business Files usually end up in a filing cabinet or on a shelf in the office or work area, but not necessarily right next to your workspace. Again, usage should determine where these will be located. If you are only using these records once a week, the cabinet or shelf can be in a back corner or out of the way, because you don't require constant access to these files. If your space is limited, don't worry if these files are not right next to your workspace or desk.

A word of caution here about security of records. If your records include information about people, for example, in client files that are arranged by personal names, then you have a class of records that may be governed by privacy laws. These records will require secure storage, limited access by employees and maintenance in a locked filing cabinet, away from public areas on your premises. Privacy issues are discussed in chapter 6.

Tip: Without a Trace

Shred your papers and reformat your disks. Take no chances with your business information. Invest in an office shredder or use a confidential disposal service to protect the privacy of your business and client information.

Permanent Files

As their name suggests, Permanent Files contain information to be kept permanently or for a long period of time. In some organizations these files are called the archives and may be kept in separate, special facilities. The main feature of this type of record is that it has value for the entire life of your business and, in some cases, long after your business operations have ceased.

Unlike most records in business, these are not destroyed. Information may travel from the Business Files into the Permanent Files. You are keeping this information because it documents the history of your business and/or because you are required by law to keep it for a long period of time.

How to Organize Permanent Files

In contrast to the Business Files, relatively few documents or records will end up in this category. However, what is kept here needs some extra care and attention. Permanent Files can include:

Agreements/Contracts
Financial Documents (summary)
Incorporation/Registration Documents
Minutes
Photographs and Graphic Material
Project, Sales or Activity Files (selected documents)
Publications (in-house newsletters, booklets, brochures, press releases)

Permanent Files should be kept somewhere safe, perhaps away from your home or office. Locations to consider include the offices of your legal and financial advisors.

For example, your incorporation documents and your minutes may stay with your lawyer. Your accountant may keep your ledgers and official financial records. Off-site commercial records storage is another option, where your records are properly stored, inventoried, protected and retrieved when necessary. The protection of these records is really important—no damp basements, dusty attics or mini-storage units, please! If you do keep them in your home or office, you might want to keep them in a fireproof vault or filing cabinet. As these records are usually few in number, a small container is likely all you will need. Storage options are discussed in chapter 5.

Tip: Keep the Gold

Be very selective when choosing materials to include in your company archives. Archival material requires special handling, housing and maintenance, and archival supplies can be costly.

Reference Files

A lot of the paper that may be cluttering up your office can probably be kept here, with the Reference Files. This material does not go into the Fingertip, Business or Permanent Files because it is of interest but not crucial to the operation of your business. The Reference Files keep track of a lot of useful and interesting information that you'd like to read or refer to at some point down the road. You did not create these documents, nor do they document the administration or functions of your business.

Examples of the type of information found in these files include newspaper and magazine clippings, brochures, offers, competitive intelligence, bulletins and professional literature. This type of information can cause small-business owners grief because it accumulates so rapidly and there is uncertainty about where to put it. If you are not sure where to put something, it sometimes seems easier not to make a decision about it at all—which is why this type of information just continues to grow in piles around the office or under the desk.

How to Organize Reference Files

Don't waste a lot of your valuable business time or space organizing these "interesting" but peripheral files. Give yourself time to read them or perhaps refer to them, but if you haven't had time or cause to look at these documents within a reasonable amount of time, *throw them out!* For most businesses a reasonable amount of time is no longer than two years from date of receipt. Use of this file group should help keep paper clutter under control and stress levels down, not increase them. Organize this information, regardless of format, by meaningful topic or subject. Categories might include:

- Books and Book Lists
- Business Trends (electronic commerce, Internet connectivity)
- Competitors
- Conferences and Conventions (including notes and handouts from those you attended)
- Course Offerings
- Industry Trends and News
- Travel Information (maps, guidebooks)

Reference-type information can be kept in a filing cabinet or where you will look at it when you have time, perhaps in the coffee break area. At some point, though, this information should be reviewed and evaluated, and you should pitch the information you decide not to keep. The rest should be filed at least once a week using the categories that you have already identified. Keep in mind that this category is where most of the paper clutter will accumulate. Get it under control and keep it under control.

Tip: Eliminate Junk Mail and Faxes

Curb or eliminate unsolicited mail and faxes by having your personal and business names removed from mailing lists. Contact direct-marketing associations to have your information removed from their members' lists. You will need to contact nonmember companies directly.

Canada
Canadian Direct Marketing Association
Do Not Mail Service
1 Concorde Gate, Suite 607
Don Mills, ON M3C 3N6
www.cdma.org

United States
Mail Preference Service
Direct Marketing Association
P.O. Box 9008
Farmingdale, NY 11735-9008
www.the-dma.org

Great Britain
Mailing Preference Service
FREEPOST 22
London, England W1E 7E2
www.dma.org.uk

Now you have the master plan. The broad categories of information presented above will live or die according to your organization's immediate and long-term needs. How to file this information—colour coding, labelling and other enhancements—is discussed in chapter 5. Many businesses keep records digitally—a whole separate issue. The records categories proposed in this book work whether the records are in paper or digital format. Electronic records are discussed in chapter 4.

When you look at your records with the four categories of Fingertip, Business, Permanent and Reference Files in mind, you start to envision a strategy for reviewing, evaluating and discarding or keeping information, by moving it along through its useful life cycle. Once you have identified your own subcategories and related topics within them, you can meet with your legal and financial advisors to confirm your strategy, particularly when it comes to deciding how long to keep records, the focus of the next chapter. But before we get to the nitty-gritty of retention details, let's take a look at an overall organizational strategy.

Paperwork: A Coping Strategy

First things first. Forget the backlog of paper clutter—for now. Instead, concentrate on dealing with information that comes into the office from this point on. You need to set up a system that allows you to effectively take charge of *current* paperwork.

All paperwork should travel in a logical path through the office, with as little handling as possible. First, incoming paperwork goes into an in-basket or other holding place until you have time to deal with it. Maybe that time only comes once every two or three days. The nature and volume of your business governs what time you have available, but don't skip the important step of making sure you have adequate time to deal with your in-basket. Making effective decisions here saves you grief and headaches (read "lost information") later on. You need to have a system in place that allows you to effectively use and store the information collected.

Items for immediate action go to the Fingertip Files. Once they have passed through the Fingertip Files, they might be transferred to the Business Files. Some information can go directly into the Business, Reference or Permanent Files. Remember, eventually most information will end up in the Permanent Files or be destroyed.

The key to dealing with paperwork is to deal with it on a regular basis and in a consistent fashion. The rule in large organizations is to file on a daily basis. A good rule of thumb, we know, but who has the time? Think of it this way: 15 minutes of reviewing and filing paperwork on a regular basis will save you a sunny Sunday cooped up inside, sorting and filing papers. Once you have your system in place, it will take, truly, only a brief amount of time to get the paperwork into the logical places. You will be able to find any piece of paper when you need it, in any crisis or calm. The reward is peace of mind.

Once the system is working with your current and incoming paperwork, tackle the backlog, which we hope you will have put away in a box to keep your office tidy. Reality tells us that you will probably need to scour your premises, leaving no place unchecked, and turn out all the paper and loose items. This will take time. How much time will depend on how many boxes you have squirreled away. Because you need to keep up with the daily flow of current information, restrict yourself to one afternoon a week to do a quick sort through the backlogged material. Start with the most recent backlog and work backwards from there, one afternoon at a time.

Assemble everything in one spot. Once you see the extent of this residual paper, take a moment to reflect on your established categories and remind yourself of the purpose for keeping business records and information.

Do a quick rough sort of the papers into three containers or boxes, labelled "to keep," "to toss" and "undecided." Do this sort as quickly as you can, and don't get distracted by interesting items you always wanted to read but had forgotten where you put or never knew you had. Now is not the time! If you cannot evaluate something immediately, put it in "undecided." Working quickly, you will winnow down the pile and have a whole lot of paper that you can discard immediately.

Throw the "to toss" pile into either the shredder or the recycling bin as soon as possible. It will probably feel good to get rid of this paper. There is nothing so satisfying as throwing out clutter that's been in your way for a long time (and probably gnawing away at your conscience, too!).

Next, gather up the "to keep" pile and divide the papers into your four broad filing categories: Fingertip, Business, Permanent and Reference. Then sort each category into the file subdivisions that you have set up. At this point, you may well create new categories (and subdivisions), based on what you find. You can add these new categories to your list.

Finally, the tough part, the "undecided" pile. Here you have to do a little more thinking and evaluating, based on whether this information is needed. Some people like to joke, "When in doubt, throw it out!" But, jokes aside, you are pondering probably because you suspect the records may have reference value. If you are really hesitating about some piece of information, create some more topics in your Reference Files, date the folder itself and file it. (When you go to file this information, you may find that you have created a duplicate reference folder, but this situation will be temporary, until the backlogged material is either used or tossed.) If you haven't touched it within a reasonable period, toss the entire folder. On the other hand, if you find that you do use this material, you can file it in the "official" reference folder. Or you may discover this information is actually relevant to your business and should be incorporated into the Business or Permanent Files. Remember, much of the material in the Reference Files can be retrieved again from other sources. Ask yourself if you must keep it.

Computerwork: A Coping Strategy

As with your paperwork, we encourage you to examine the contents of your computer files with the same kind of concentration, focusing on what you need now for the daily work of your business. Without a logical filing system, your computer files are likely the same chaotic mix as your paper files. So, file cleanup involves a similar strategy.

First, separate out the current information from the completed or inactive information. It is usually easiest to create a directory on your hard drive for your active records, as well as a temporary directory for unneeded information. It might be easier to think this through by printing out a copy of your existing file directories, software programs and files within these programs. Then ask yourself the same questions as you did with the paper records. Do you need this for administrative, financial or operational reasons? Do you need it for legal or regulatory purposes? Does it have reference value? Does it have historic or archival value? Do you need to keep it here, with the active files? Do you need it at all? Move through the various programs, identify the inactive information, and move this information to your holding or storage directory on your computer hard drive.

Identify your current projects or activities. These will probably match the categories you have already established for your paper-based information. Use the same four broad categories to set up your active directory—Fingertip, Business, Permanent and Reference.

Within each of these categories, establish the same topics or subjects you have already created for the paper files. Subdivide them accordingly. Ensure that for each document ("file") you create on the computer, you follow a logical naming system, and that you place the documents in the appropriate directory. If you choose to develop a coded system for your paper files (more on this subject to follow), use the same codes for your computer directory setup.

As your need for the electronic documents diminishes, move them from your active directory to your storage directory. Do this on a regular basis, just as you file and review your paper filing categories. (For details on the management of electronic records and backing up of data, see chapter 4.) If you take on new business, new clients or new projects, set up your directory to include these new items in the same way that you are setting up your paper files to accommodate the hard-copy records.

Don't forget about your e-mail directories. Managing e-mail messages is probably the biggest daily electronic-records management problem. Be sure to review your electronic-mail directories. Frequently, e-mail is opened, read and left in the electronic "in-basket" (just like the unsorted piles of paper around the office). Review, delete or file your e-mail messages, including attachments, where they belong.

Create a printed copy of your directory and file structures. File the paper copy with your list of paper files at the front of the filing cabinet drawer. Either merge this list with the list of paper files or keep two separate lists.

Alphabetic or Coded Labelling

Getting back to the overall office filing system, once you've decided on your business-specific categories, your next decision is how to label each folder, container or computer directory so that you will know what should be filed within it. Two typical approaches are to use an alphabetic descriptor or name, or to use a numeric or alphanumeric code to represent the contents of a file.

An alphabetic label is a meaningful word or phrase that clearly describes what should be filed in the container. Alphabetic labels include personal names, geographic locations, and subjects or topics. Numeric or alphanumeric codes use a number or combination of number and letters to represent the file contents. Codes show the links between file categories and group related categories, whereas the alphabetic system does not. Examples of numeric codes include pre-existing numbers, for instance, policy numbers or customer numbers.

Numeric or alphanumeric codes will require some sort of index to relate the contents to the codes, so that you or your staff will know what to file where. It's hard to remember what the numbers mean, even if you are the one who sets up these categories. Use your computer to establish and update an alphabetic list either in a database or on a spreadsheet.

Consider carefully the choice to use an alphabetic or

numeric coded system. A simple alphabetic system is probably enough to start with, particularly if your volume of records is low. If you anticipate that your volume of records will increase, you might want to expand your alphabetic records lists to include a numeric or alphanumeric code. For example, you could enhance your *Finance* category by making it a "500" series. Then you could use individual numbers within the 500 range to designate various financial functions, for example, "510 – Accounting"; "520 – Accounts Payable"; "540 – Banking"; and so on. Use numeric codes only if you know your system is going to grow large enough that the individual alphabetic titles are not meaningful on their own or the number of subdivisions is unwieldy.

Tip: Create a Filing Key

Don't get locked out of your files. Be sure your file key or index is the first item in your file drawer. To make your index even more accessible, print it on brightly coloured paper.

Some organizations end up with a combination of alphabetic and numeric codes. For example, a small engineering firm might decide to use numeric codes for its projects. Each project would be given a project number, and all correspondence, drawings and records related to that project would be filed by project number. An alphabetic system would be used concurrently to keep track of administrative records. The administrative records would be filed by topic alphabetically, the easiest filing method for most people.

Records Management Software

If you feel comfortable using computing technology, a records management software program will provide you with an electronic tool to manage the life cycle of your information. Just as financial software provides you with tools to better process and track financial transactions, these software programs help you manage your information. For example, you can prepare detailed file lists, assign classification codes to record, catalogue your records, create file labels, track file folder or stored records locations, or program records destruction. More recently, these programs have expanded to include the management of electronic records in their diverse software programs and to provide basic functionality for mounting information on the Internet. No matter which program you select, most records management software programs enable you to speed up or improve manual processes associated with records management.

Keep in mind that many of these programs were designed to manage large volumes of records, and if you are a small organization or one with few records, these software programs may be more complex and offer more functionality than you require. However, consider using one as the number of your records increases and as your systems require more processing.

Most records management software programs have websites on the Internet and may have demonstration modules that you can download to test. The Association for Records Managers and Administrators, ARMA International, produces an annual summary of the software programs available. We've included information about ARMA International in Appendix B.

Alphabetic Office Filing System

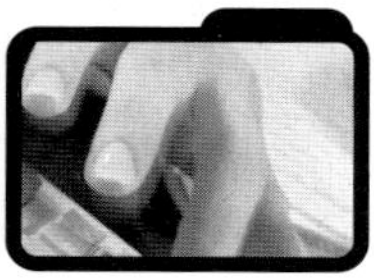

Fingertip Files

Calendar (filed by date)
- Appointments
- Bills to Pay
- Bring-Forward Information
- Callback Information
- Special Event Notices
- Tickets
- To-Do Lists
- Travel Arrangements

Contacts/Organizations
- Business Cards
- Client Contact Information
- Newsletters
- Schedules

Receipts
- Automobile/Transportation Receipts
- Bank Machine/ATM Transaction Receipts
- Cash Transaction Receipts
- Courier and Shipping Receipts
- Credit Card Receipts
- Parking Receipts
- Petty Cash Receipts
- Project/Expense-Related Receipts

Business Files

Administrative Files

Administration (or Office Administration)
- Insurance
- Legal Matters
- Meetings
- Memberships
- Publicity/Public Relations
- Travel

Equipment, Supplies and Services
- Catalogues, Manuals, Price Lists
- Computers—Hardware
- Computers—Software
- Computers—Network
- Furniture and Equipment
- Postal, Courier and Freight
- Stationery
- Vehicle(s)

Finance
- Accounting System and Procedures
- Accounts Payable
- Accounts Receivable
- Banking
- Credit Cards
- Expenses
- Financial Statements
- Salaries and Wages
- Suppliers
- Taxation

Personnel and Staffing
- General Personnel Matters
- Benefits
- Contractors and Subcontractors
- Employees
- Health and Safety
- Hiring and Recruitment
- Training

at a Glance

Business Files cont'd

Administrative Files cont'd

Premises

- Lease
- Maintenance
- Utilities

Operational Files

- Business Plan
- Customers/Clients
- Inventory
- Marketing
- Presentations and Seminars
- Product Sales
- Projects
- Supplies

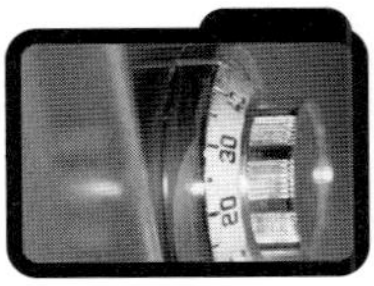

Permanent Files

- Agreements/Contracts
- Financial Documents
- Incorporation/Registration Documents
- Minutes
- Photographs and Graphic Material
- Project, Sales or Activity Files
- Publications

Reference Files

- Books and Book Lists
- Business Trends
- Competitors
- Conferences and Conventions
- Course Offerings
- Industry Trends and News
- Travel Information

Coded Office Filing System at a

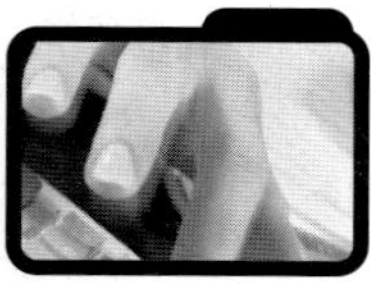

Fingertip Files (0–999)

100 – Calendar (filed by date)
- Appointments
- Bills to Pay
- Bring-Forward Information
- Callback Information
- Special Event Notices
- Tickets
- To-Do Lists
- Travel Arrangements

200 – Contacts/Organizations
- 210 – Business Cards
- 220 – Client Contact Information
- 230 – Newsletters
- 240 – Schedules

300 – Receipts
- 310 – Automobile/Transportation Receipts
- 320 – Bank Machine/ATM Transaction Receipts
- 330 – Cash Transaction Receipts
- 340 – Courier and Shipping Receipts
- 350 – Credit Card Receipts
- 360 – Parking Receipts
- 370 – Petty Cash Receipts
- 380 – Project/Expense-Related Receipts

400–999 (for future expansion of categories)

Business Files (1000–2999)

Administrative Files (1000–1999)

1000 – Administration (or Office Administration)
- 1010 – Insurance
- 1020 – Legal Matters
- 1030 – Meetings
- 1040 – Memberships
- 1050 – Publicity/Public Relations
- 1060 – Travel

1100 – Equipment, Supplies and Services
- 1110 – Catalogues, Manuals, Price Lists
- 1120 – Computers—Hardware
- 1130 – Computers—Software
- 1140 – Computers—Network
- 1150 – Furniture and Equipment
- 1160 – Postal, Courier and Freight
- 1170 – Stationery
- 1180 – Vehicle(s)

1200 – Finance
- 1210 – Accounting System and Procedures
- 1220 – Accounts Payable
- 1225 – Accounts Receivable
- 1230 – Banking
- 1240 – Credit Cards
- 1250 – Expenses
- 1260 – Financial Statements
- 1270 – Salaries and Wages
- 1280 – Suppliers
- 1290 – Taxation

1300 – Personnel and Staffing
- 1310 – General Personnel Matters
- 1320 – Benefits
- 1330 – Contractors and Subcontractors
- 1340 – Employees
- 1350 – Health and Safety
- 1360 – Hiring and Recruitment
- 1370 – Training

Business Files cont'd

Administrative Files cont'd

1400 – Premises

- 1410 – Lease
- 1420 – Maintenance
- 1430 – Utilities

Operational Files (2000–2900)

2000 – Business Plan

- 2010 – Financial Plan
- 2020 – Operational Plan

2100 – Customers/Clients

- 2100 – B Brown, Jane
- 2100 – S Smith, John

2200 – Inventory

- 2210 – Inventory—Raw Materials
- 2220 – Inventory—Finished Products

2300 – Marketing

2400 – Presentations and Seminars

2500 – Product Sales

2600 – Projects

2700 – Supplies

Permanent Files (3000–3999)

3000 – Agreements/Contracts
3100 – Financial Documents
3200 – Incorporation/Registration Documents
3300 – Minutes
3400 – Photographs and Graphic Material
3500 – Project, Sales or Activity Files
3600 – Publications

Reference Files (4000–4999)

4000 – Books and Book Lists
4100 – Business Trends
4200 – Competitors
4300 – Conferences and Conventions
4400 – Course Offerings
4500 – Industry Trends and News
4600 – Travel Information

3
For How Long and Why?

SETTING UP AND USING THE FILING SYSTEM DESCRIBED HERE GETS you started on the way to total information control. Setting up and implementing a *retention schedule*—a blueprint for how long you keep information—ensures that your control will continue as your business grows and prospers. A retention schedule ensures that the volume of information doesn't become unmanageable. Once you have organized your records into your categories (and are filing and finding information as easily as we have predicted you will), the next question you will be asking yourself is "How long do I have to keep these records?"

Let's review the four broad categories of records: Fingertip Files, Business Files, Permanent Files and Reference Files. These broad categories ensure easy access and retrieval, but there is also an implicit time frame associated with each. Fingertip Files contain transitory or time-sensitive information that, once used, is either discarded or transferred to the Business or Permanent Files. The Business Files generally contain information needed for a number years, perhaps as long as projects are active and employees remain with the company. Permanent Files, as their name implies, have a very long or permanent lifetime; consequently, they are pretty straightforward to deal with. Reference Files, because the information in them is external or "of interest" only, can and should be discarded after a defined time period.

(If you haven't used the information in a particular reference file within two years, get rid of it. Chances are slim to none that you will ever refer to it, and it's costing you maintenance time and space to keep.)

As we begin to examine these groups more closely, we hope you will see a pattern emerge, with the groups of records associated with particular retention time periods. We hope the issue of when to discard information will start to appear more rational and that the "keepers" among you will feel comfortable with the notion of applying retention principles and guidelines. Think of the guidelines set out in this chapter as rules that will help you deal with incoming information, manage existing information and keep information under control.

Some of the retention guidelines will depend only on your own needs and level of comfort with paperwork. Other retention guidelines are imposed on your business by government or regulatory bodies whose jurisdiction includes telling you how long you must keep and be able to produce records. What follows are general principles, as well as some guidance on regulations. No two businesses are alike, however. Your business may have some specific requirements that these guidelines do not take into account. Any final actions you take to destroy or remove records should be verified by your professional advisors.

Another important matter to consider here is what information is critical or vital to the running of your business. This information may not necessarily be permanent but may, for a time, be essential for you to operate your business. These are your *vital business records*. Examples include your current accounts receivable, incorporation documents and current contracts. Only a few records are classified as vital. Copies of these should be stored elsewhere in case of an emergency such as a fire or a flood on your premises. Security matters are discussed in chapter 6.

Tip: Mark Your Vital Records

Identify your vital records on both your master file list and the actual file folders or disks kept on your premises with a unique identifier such as a sticker, for example, a red dot. The red dot will be easy to spot if you need to retrieve folders or disks in a hurry.

Retention Principles

In chapter 1, we discussed the differing values that information can have for your business. These values—administrative or financial, operational, legal or regulatory, reference, historic or archival—are the basis for determining how long to keep information. How long information should be kept is its *retention period.*

Most information readily fits into a life cycle that has three phases:

- *active phase:* the information is current, needed for daily work or decision-making, and must be close at hand to maximize efficiency and productivity (and save stress!)
- *inactive phase:* the information has passed the immediate use or need phase and is no longer referenced but must be retained to fulfill some regulation or business requirement. At this stage, inactive records can be boxed and shipped off the premises to the care of a commercial records storage company. Clutter is reduced on the premises, freeing up

valuable space, but the records are safe and retrievable if the auditors or authorities require you to produce them (or that cancelled project comes back to life).

- *final disposition phase:* the information is no longer needed for business purposes. At this point one of two things can happen. Either your information will be destroyed because it has no further value to your business, or it will be transferred to your designated safe-storage facility for permanent retention. Consider these permanent records your company archives.

These retention principles give all your business information a life cycle. When the life cycle of the information ends, the information has no value, and most of it is destroyed. Putting retention principles into action is key in maintaining good control over your business records.

By applying retention principles in a logical and systematic way, you are also providing yourself with a defensible system of records management. What do we mean by *defensible?* We mean that you can defend your information management practices. You will have a regular and routine practice of records disposal that reflects a well-thought-out rationale.

As you review the suggested guidelines on the following pages, create your own retention schedule or plan. A retention schedule is easiest to manage if you put the retention instructions on your list of files. After you have completed your review and analysis, regularly apply the process of moving records on. Once you have reviewed and created a records retention framework based on appropriate reasons, you should then apply it in a systematic way. This ensures you are employing retention principles as part of the regular and usual course of your business activities, and are not destroying records in an arbitrary manner. This documented and practised routine provides your defence, possibly a legal or regulatory one, should you ever be challenged about your records disposal.

Retention Guidelines

As records managers and information specialists, we work with large organizations whose record-keeping requirements often involve extensive regulatory research, because of the operational complexity and geographic location of their business. You, however, are probably working in a smaller, more manageable setting. Even so, we recommend that you do a little homework in the area of retention guidelines and determine what particular regulations affect your business. After you read our general information, check out the resources in Appendix B that point to sources and authorities whose regulations might apply to your operations. Don't feel overwhelmed at this stage; take it a step at a time. After reading our guidelines, you will become familiar with what kinds of questions to ask your legal advisor or accountant.

Tip: Get the Low-Down on Laws

Regardless of jurisdiction, regulations usually govern records documenting income tax, corporate tax, employees, and heath and safety. There may be other regulations depending on the nature of your business. Don't be afraid to ask questions about requirements—as a business operator, you need to know.

Depending upon where you live, you will have some obvious authorities to consult. In Canada, municipal, provincial and federal authorities may have some retention requirements that affect your record-keeping practices. Likewise, in the U.S., local, state and federal authorities may have specific requirements. In the United Kingdom, check with specific agencies such as the Inland Revenue Service, which covers taxation issues.

Where to start? Begin with the local authorities and progress to the higher level of authority on the recommendation of the lower body. Frequently, these agencies will have the same or similar requirements. For example, in Canada most provincial taxation regulations mirror those established by Revenue Canada. There are publications and, increasingly, websites that you can check for retention guidelines for business documents. Check out Appendix B for lists of government authorities for further information, including on-line access to government sites. The appendix brings together lists of common sources to check and also provides you with further readings.

You may also have to pay attention to the format in which records must be kept. Until recently, most regulatory bodies expected or required that the requisite business records be retained in paper format or on microfilm. More recently, as electronic information has become the widespread tool of business communication, some bodies have updated their requirements to permit electronic formats as the "official" record. Usually, the regulations for length of retention will tell you in what format you need to keep records. Most experts will tell you that the format of the records is not so important a consideration as your management practices associated with the records. For example, are your procedures written down for all to follow? Do you annually purge your records? As one of our associates says, "Document what you do, then do what you document."

Now let's revisit our four major categories—Fingertip, Business, Permanent and Reference Files—and look at them from the perspective of how long the information should be kept.

Fingertip Files

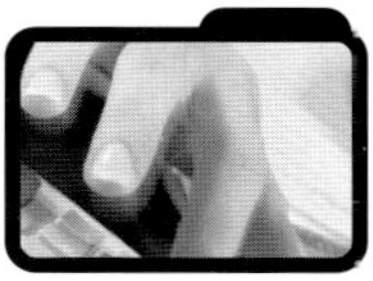

Remember our earlier reason for creating this group of records—all the information in this category is time-sensitive and, by its very nature, will be required for action on a specific date. After you have completed the action, the documents or records will move into one of your other record groups or be discarded. (If you let records accumulate in this category, pretty quickly the clutter will begin. You'll lose the flexible and retrievable features that were intended when you put the information here in the first place.) For ease of access and retrieval, the Fingertip Files are subdivided into the three broad categories *Calendar, Contacts/Organizations* and *Receipts*. See Appendix A for instructions on how to set up the Fingertip Files.

Calendar

Discard or file after use

Items kept here provide information or documents needed on a specific day. Once the information is used, it can be either destroyed or, if necessary, filed in one of the other categories, Business, Permanent or Reference Files.

Retain your appointment registry or date calendar for

the current calendar year. If you also use your appointment calendar to record expenses or track auto mileage, move this information into the financial files within your Business Files. If a ticket is also a receipt, move it to your financial files. Same goes for any travel receipts. Examples of information to be kept in the *Calendar* section include:

Appointments	*Current year only*
Bills to Pay	*Until paid, then transfer to Business Files*
Bring-Forward Information	*Until date of action, then transfer to appropriate records category*
Callback Information	*After date of call, update contact information, then discard*
Special Event Notices	*Discard after use or date of event*
Tickets	*Discard after use unless a receipt, then transfer to Business Files*
To-Do Lists	*Discard after use*
Travel Arrangements	*Discard after use*

Contacts/Organizations

Current only

Replace or revise this information once you receive more current information. Business cards, phone numbers, mailing and e-mail addresses are all used to make contact with people or businesses. Outdated contact information cannot do that for you, so get rid of it. Schedules for travel and other activities are also date-sensitive. For reference purposes, you might want to keep your client information in two places—a second copy in your operational Business Files in the client or project categories. Examples of the type of information found in this section include:

Business Cards	*Current only; discard when updated or replaced*
Client Contact Information	*Current only; discard when updated or replaced*
Newsletters	*Current only; discard or transfer to Reference Files when replaced*
Schedules	*Current only; discard when replaced*

Receipts

Selectively retain

You will collect a wide variety of receipts documenting various financial transactions. Many receipts collected here are from out-of-pocket, personal expenditures that must be reimbursed by the business. We distinguish between the types of receipts and where they go because they have different values to the business.

Automobile/Transportation Receipts	*Until reimbursed and/or verified, then transfer to Business Files*
Bank Machine/ATM Transaction Receipts	*Until verified by statement, then shred*
Cash Transaction Receipts	*Until reimbursed and/or verified, then transfer to Business Files*
Courier and Shipping Receipts	*Until reimbursed and/or verified, then transfer to Business Files*
Credit Card Receipts	*Until verified by statement, then transfer to Business Files*
Parking Receipts	*Until reimbursed and/or verified, then transfer to Business Files*

Petty Cash Receipts	*Until reimbursed, then transfer to Business Files*
Project/Expense-Related Receipts	*Until reimbursed and/or verified, then transfer to Business Files*

Receipts document financial transactions, and once you've used them for initial confirmation, verification and reimbursement of out-of-pocket expenditures, they will be required as part of your financial record keeping—hence the recommendation that most of these receipts in the Fingertip Files be moved into your Business Files. Retain credit card receipts in your Business Files if required for proof of purchase or for warranty purposes. Your accountant or bookkeeper has probably already specified into what accounting categories or codes these should be batched, as part of the paper or audit trail required by most authorities governing businesses. Alternatively, you may set up categories according to accounting software packages or the reporting categories on your taxation reporting forms.

Business Files

As discussed earlier, it helps to think of your Business Files as two types—administrative and operational. The distinction is useful for determining how long to keep them. Generally speaking, administrative-type records are found in most types of organizations. As a result, there are often external guidelines on how long to keep them, usually from the government agencies or regulatory bodies that oversee functions such as taxation, employee relations and worker safety, landlord-tenant relations and so on. Depending upon the nature of your business, there may or may not be external bodies with requirements affecting your operational records. Remember, when evaluating your records for their value to the business, you must also consider what outside agencies or laws may govern your retention practices.

Administrative Files

Administration (or Office Administration)

Insurance

Keep here all information about the insurance policies your company holds (excepting insurance for personnel).

Policies:	Automobile	*Until expired or replaced*
	General Liability/Operating	*Until expired or replaced*
	Premises/Contents	*Until expired or replaced*
Claims		*Until settled and all limitation periods have expired*

Retain insurance policy information until coverage expires or the policy is updated and replaced. Most insurance policies' coverage is annual. As for insurance claims, file here information about claims initiated by your company against others or claims initiated by others against your company. Retain any claim-related records until all claims have been settled and any legal limitation periods have expired or until you have been advised by your insurance carrier that it is okay to discard them. Insurance for personnel—such as health or dental insurance, accident and disability insurance, or group life insurance—should go into *Personnel and Staffing* records.

Legal Matters

Keep here records of any legal matters involving your company, such as legal opinions and decisions, administration of oaths, references to legal challenges and related matters. Keep original legal documents, such as deeds or leases, in your Permanent Files. You might want to keep photocopies here for quick reference, especially if some of your permanent records are kept off-site and are not easily retrieved.

Legal Matters	*As long as required to protect the legal rights and obligations of your company*

You may want to selectively retain some of the information and transfer this to a permanent file for future operating reference. In other words (and we hope this never happens to you), if your company is sued, after the matter is resolved you may still wish to refer to the related information for future planning. No doubt your legal advisor will also retain information about these matters. Check with them before discarding *any* information in this category.

Meetings

Keep here minutes or notes of staff meetings, filed by date of meeting, for the current year plus the previous year.

Minutes	*Current year plus one, then transfer to Permanent Files*

The minutes of most meetings are considered documentation of the history of the company in addition to resolving matters of day-to-day concern. The recommendation here is to keep minutes from the current year plus one year past close at hand, then transfer the records to the Permanent Files.

Memberships

Keep here the routine information regarding your memberships. This includes applications, dues, meeting notices, newsletters and related correspondence associated with memberships in community, service, professional and other organizations associated with your business. Financial information, such as dues receipts, should be retained in your financial files.

Organization #1	*Current year only; selectively retain*
Organization #2	*Current year only; selectively retain*

Information in this category may also be divided between the Fingertip Files and the Business Files. In other words, the meeting notice that arrives in your mailbox will be noted in your calendar, and the notice with directions and the time of the meeting will be filed in the Fingertip Files for the day of the event. After the event, you might wish to keep the information for the current year in the membership file. Financial information associated with your membership should be filed with your financial files and retained until all audit, tax and other requirements have been met. You may also wish to retain permanently some key information documenting your active participation or achievements in these organizations for archival purposes.

Publicity/Public Relations

Keep here advertising, brochures, printed notices, or any information that you prepare for clients or for public distribution. This category includes original artwork or commissioned materials. If you prepare this type of material for projects, then subdivide this category by project name or title. For example, if you conduct a workshop entitled "Getting Organized for Back to School," then create a specific file for the publicity materials for this event. This category is for publicity materials only. Other materials, such as course notes or financial information (except receipts), should be filed in the project file within your operational Business Files.

Publicity Projects/Materials	*Until updated or replaced; file one copy in Permanent Files*
Publicity—External	*Current year only, then transfer to Permanent Files*

It's a good idea to immediately place a copy of any publicity materials you produce, including the artwork or creative items that are part of the final product, in a permanent file for archival purposes. Discard all but the final draft of any work in progress, unless you felt the drafts told a story independent of the final product. Some businesspeople keep a working copy of their materials as a source of ideas for the next brochure or advertisement, in addition to the copies that are being kept to give away to customers or others. You can also keep publicity about your company that is externally generated in this category or create a subdivision entitled "Publicity—External," in which you file copies of all external articles, photographs and other information.

Travel

Keep here information about travel arrangements and reservations, hotel and car rental brochures, and related items. If you receive bonus points either directly linked to your travel or through your use of a particular bonus program, keep the records here. Tickets themselves will go in the Fingertip Files until you use them. Travel expense records should be filed with your financial files. You may want to keep all your arrangement information for two years so that you can refer back when making future arrangements.

Travel Arrangements	*Current year plus one, then discard*
Travel Bonus Programs	*Current only; discard as updated*
Travel Brochures	*Until updated or replaced, then discard*

Equipment, Supplies and Services

All information in these filing subdivisions is related to the operation of, functioning of and warranties for your office equipment, furniture and services. Any purchasing information, such as quotes, shipping information and receipts, should be retained in your financial files.

Catalogues, Manuals, Price Lists

Keep here the equipment and suppliers' catalogues, manuals and price lists that you use for your business. We suggest you consolidate this information here for two reasons. First, you can quickly scan prices and compare products. Second, it is easier to remove and update catalogues and price lists when they are all in one spot rather than filed by supplier. Information about the individual suppliers, including ordering arrangements, should be filed separately under "Suppliers" in the *Finance* category.

Catalogues, Manuals, Price Lists	*Until updated or replaced, then discard*

Computers—Hardware

Keep here information about your office computers, including purchasing specifications (receipts go to the financial files), technical manuals, warranties and guarantees. If you have more than one computer or workstation, you should have a separate file for each.

Computer #1	*For one year past sale or disposition (by you)*
Computer #2	*For one year past sale or disposition (by you)*

Although computer technology is constantly changing, you should retain as current information all records associated with your computers for as long as you own them. Keep the information for one year after you sell or otherwise dispose of the hardware to satisfy any accounting requirements you might have.

Computers—Software

Keep here information about your office computer software, including correspondence, warranties, licensing agreements and related information. You need to keep this information for as long as you are using the program. You can also file here original program disks and manuals. (On the other hand, you might prefer to keep the actual program disks in a safe place, perhaps off-site.) We discuss backup program information in chapter 4. As with computer hardware information, you should retain software documentation one year after disposition to satisfy any accounting requirements.

Software Program #1	*Until software is updated, replaced or disposed of*
Software Program #2	*Until software is updated, replaced or disposed of*

Tip: Coping with Computer Information

Remember, you need computer hardware and software to read or use digital information. For as long as you retain information produced using computers and software, you also need the version of the software that produced the information and the compatible hardware to read or reprint it. These are more complex needs than with paper records, where, so long as you can read the paper document, your information is accessible and usable.

Computers—Network

Keep here any information related to your computer network, that is, the hardware and software associated with running an office computer network. Again, it's wise to retain this information a further year after disposition to satisfy any accounting requirements. Information about suppliers, including the telephone company or Internet service provider, should be filed under "Suppliers" in the *Finance* category.

Network Computers	*Until sold or otherwise disposed of*
Network Programs	*Until updated or disposed of*

Furniture and Equipment

Keep here any information about the furniture and equipment you acquire and use, excepting the purchase receipts or payment arrangements (for example, loans or leases), which are financial records.

Equipment (tape recorder, camera)	*Until sold or otherwise disposed of*
Furniture (desk, bookcase)	*Until sold or otherwise disposed of*

If you have few items of furniture and equipment, keep it simple and keep information all together in one file. Depending upon the number of items, you might want to establish separate files for each item or group of items, for example, by equipment type or by office location, if you occupy several sites. Keep all purchase information in your financial files. Retain records a further year after disposition to satisfy any accounting requirements.

Postal, Courier and Freight

Keep here records about the services you use for mail and delivery. Include account information (but not receipts or bills), agreements, lists of services, rate sheets and related records. File information by company name if you use more than one company for any one service. Retain waybills or shipping advice only until confirmed on statements.

Courier Service	*Until updated or services no longer used*
Freight Service	*Until updated or services no longer used*
Postal Information	*Until updated or services no longer used*

Stationery

Keep here all information relating to your office stationery and related supplies, including the printing and production of your letterhead, business cards, logos and forms. Don't forget to include an actual sample of your letterhead or business cards. You'll probably want to keep the samples to document the history of your business. Purchase receipts are financial records and should be retained with your accounts payable records.

Stationery	*Until updated or replaced; selectively retain*

Vehicle(s)

Keep here all information related to your company vehicles, including trucks, vans, trailers, boats and airplanes. The licensing, warranty, maintenance, mileage, fuel and related information may be filed by individual vehicle, if you have a number of different types of vehicles or a fleet to manage. Receipts for purchase, lease or operating expenses associated with the vehicles should be retained in your financial files.

Vehicle #1 (Automobile)	*Until vehicle is disposed of*
Vehicle #2 (Truck)	*Until vehicle is disposed of*
Vehicle #3 (Boat)	*Until vehicle is disposed of*

Finance

This section of the Business Files represents a block of information that is, most likely, critical to your company's operations. Also, information in this section is subject to external regulation of some sort, whether for tax, audit, financial reporting or general accountability purposes. Here we provide general commonsense guidelines, but we urge you to review this section with your own financial advisors to ensure that you comply with specific jurisdictional requirements that may apply to your business.

Accounting System and Procedures

Keep here all the records associated with your company accounting system. This includes your chart of accounts, advice from your accounting firm and related records. Whether your accounting system is set up in a paper ledger, on specific computer software or at your accountant's office, this category in your files is only for information *about* your accounting system and procedures. If your accounting needs are minimal, this particular file might include only basic financial information from outside agencies such as taxation authorities.

Accounting Advice	*Current year plus one, then transfer to Permanent Files*
Accounting Codes	*Until updated or replaced*
Accounting Procedures	*Until updated or replaced*
Accounting Software System	*Until updated or replaced*
Accounting Software System Reports	*Current year plus one, then transfer to Permanent Files*

If you use accounting software, the financial transactions of your company will be recorded and retained in the accounting software. Follow the guidelines of your accountant for how long to keep the software system data. We recommend keeping the annual final copies of your general ledger and related reports permanently, because these records provide a picture of the financial state and progress of your company.

The source documents for transactions recorded in the software should be filed in the accounts payable and accounts receivable files (discussed below). Keep the accounting software system disk and manuals with your other computer software and related materials.

Accounts Payable

Keep here records relating to accounts payable, the money your company owes to others. This will be the file where you keep track of paid bills. Remember, you have placed unpaid bills in the *Calendar* section of the Fingertip Files. Once you pay a bill, you should file it in "Accounts Payable."

If you have a series of regular accounts to pay, such as telephone or office rent, you should create a separate file within this category for each of these accounts. On the other hand, if your payables are few in number or irregular, you can simply keep them all together in one file. Your accountant might suggest that you file your payables according to account codes that he or she sets up in your general ledger.

Accounts Payable (by supplier or individual)	*Current year plus one, then transfer to storage and retain until no longer required for audit or taxation purposes*

This group of records has a finite life cycle, after which they can be destroyed. Check with your financial advisor or taxation authorities to determine when you are permitted to destroy these files.

Tip: Don't Get Personal

If a particular bill covers both personal and business use, retain it as a business record in your "Accounts Payable" file. You are probably keeping this bill or statement to document a business tax deduction rather than a personal one.

Accounts Receivable

May your accounts receivable files be always overflowing! Keep here the records of money owed to your company. Records in this category document who owes you money and when payment has been received.

Depending on the volume of your records, you might want to split the records into two files—receivables outstanding and receivables paid. Or, as with accounts payable, your accountant might suggest you file your receivables according to account codes that he or she sets up in your general ledger.

Accounts Receivable (by supplier or individual)	*Current year plus one, then transfer to storage and retain until no longer required for audit or taxation purposes*

You might have an electronic accounting system to track your accounts receivable and produce records such as invoices and reports. If this is the case, you might have only a printed copy of a report from your accounting system in this file category.

Like payables, this group of records has a finite life cycle, after which it can be destroyed. Check with your financial advisor or taxation authorities to determine when you are permitted to destroy these files.

Banking

Keep here records about your company banking arrangements as well as bank accounts. Within these records, you might also have information about banking services, signing authorities, fees and agreements, banking supplies, bank statements or books, and cancelled cheques. You might also have mortgage or loan and credit information filed in this category, by the name of the financial institution that extends the credit to your company. You may be able to put all of the records in one file. However, depending upon the complexity of your financial relationships and situations, it might be necessary to subdivide them into separate files by the type of relationship. After two years, all account, loan and mortgage information should be transferred to storage until no longer required for audit or taxation purposes.

Bank/Financial Institution—General Information		*Until updated or services no longer used*
Bank/Financial Institution—Account Information		
	Account #1	*Current year plus one, then transfer to storage and retain until no longer required for audit or taxation purposes*
	Account #2	*Current year plus one, then transfer to storage and retain until no longer required for audit or taxation purposes*
Bank/Financial Institution—Loan		*Until discharged, then transfer to storage and retain until no longer required for audit or taxation purposes*
Bank/Financial Institution—Mortgage		*Until discharged, then transfer to storage and retain until no longer required for audit or taxation purposes*

Credit Cards

Keep here the agreements and arrangements for credit cards, plus correspondence, supplies and statements from credit card companies or financial institutions. The statements here should include receipts from credit card transactions that were initially collected in the Fingertip Files, then verified against the statements. Technically, a credit card statement is another account payable, and you might choose to keep it in the "Accounts Payable" category. However, to track and document your obligations to the holder of the credit card, it is simpler to file the records in their own category.

Credit Cards		
All-Purpose:	Correspondence	*Current year plus one*
	General Information	*Until updated or replaced*
	Statements/Receipts	*Current year plus one, then transfer to storage and retain until no longer required for audit or taxation purposes*
Gas/Petrol:	Correspondence	*Current year plus one*
	General Information	*Until updated or replaced*
	Statements/Receipts	*Current year plus one, then transfer to storage and retain until no longer required for audit or taxation purposes*
Store Card:	Correspondence	*Current year plus one*
	General Information	*Until updated or replaced*
	Statements/Receipts	*Current year plus one, then transfer to storage and retain until no longer required for audit or taxation purposes*

Expenses

Keep here records relating to the reimbursement from the company of out-of-pocket personal expenses for travel, automobile use or purchases related to the business. If you have few transactions to document, keep them together in one file. Information in this category is technically another type of account payable. However, since these payments are reimbursements rather than payments for services rendered, we recommend that you file the information and receipts here.

Expenses—Petty Cash	*Current year plus one, then transfer to storage and retain until no longer required for audit or taxation purposes*
Expenses—Travel	*Current year plus one, then transfer to storage and retain until no longer required for audit or taxation purposes*
Expenses—Vehicle	*Current year plus one, then transfer to storage and retain until no longer required for audit or taxation purposes*

Financial Statements

Keep here the periodic and annual financial statements that summarize all company financial activities.

Financial Statements	*Current year plus one, then transfer to Permanent Files*

Salaries and Wages

Keep here information related to the administration and payment of salaries and wages to employees of the company. (Fees paid to contractors and subcontractors are considered accounts payable rather than salaries and wages.) Information in this category will include general matters relating to the administration and payment of salaries and wages, such as notices from authorities, as well as the individual payroll records of staff.

If you have an electronic accounting system, the pay register will be a file within the electronic system. Keep here the printed reports from the system. You might wish keep selected payroll records to document the history of your company. Some jurisdictions may require you to retain employee pay information for a period of time after employment ceases.

Salaries and Wages:	General Information	*Until updated or replaced*
Payroll:	General Information	*Until updated or replaced; selectively retain*
	Staff	*Current year plus one, then transfer to storage and retain until no longer required for audit or taxation purposes*

Suppliers

Keep here ordering information, statements and correspondence from suppliers of routine office goods and services.

Suppliers (alphabetical by name)	*Current year plus one, then destroy*

Taxation

Taxes—the bane of the small-business owner! Although it feels as if there are too many taxes to keep track of, this area is usually quite clearly defined, both in terms of what records to keep and for how long to keep them. You will need to become familiar with taxation laws that govern your business. Your accountant will know these. Also, use Appendix B to help you get started in locating these requirements on your own.

Keep here records about the various taxes or fees that your business must collect or remit to various authorities.

Taxes Collected (by year)	*Current year plus one, then transfer to storage and retain until all audit or reporting periods are complete*
Taxes Paid (by year)	*Current year plus one, then transfer to storage and retain until all audit or reporting periods are complete*

Your business may be obliged to collect more than one type of tax or fee for one or more taxation authorities. For ease of record keeping and simplicity of remittance to authorities, subdivide these categories according to either the type of tax or the authority (municipal fees, provincial/state tax or federal tax). For example, a gardening or landscaping business might be obliged to collect an environmental fee or tax for products sold, in addition to other applicable taxes. The business owner could set up a file in the taxation category labelled "Taxes Collected—Environmental Fees 2001."

Make up a new file for each year that you have taxes to track. If you follow our guideline for keeping the current year plus one, you will have two files in your cabinet. Then it's a simple matter to take the oldest file folder and move it to storage, without having to sort out which papers you want to keep on hand. When all obligations for keeping this file have passed, destroy the folder and its contents without having to handle paper again.

Personnel and Staffing

Next to the *Finance* section (depending upon the size of your business), the *Personnel and Staffing* section of the Business Files probably represents a block of information that is the most critical to a company's operations. On the other hand, if you have no employees, you may want to skip ahead to the discussion about *Premises* on page 74. Information in this section may be subject to external regulation of some sort, whether for compliance to employment laws or to assist your employees with their rights. An employee's pension eligibility or access to benefits may depend upon *your* record keeping. We discuss in general commonsense practices, but again we urge you to review this section with your own advisors to ensure that you comply with whatever jurisdictional issues apply to your company.

As with other types of records in your company, if you only have one employee, with few records generated, you will probably keep all this information in one file. However, as your business grows, you may need to expand your personnel records to encompass the following more detailed subdivisions.

General Personnel Matters

Keep here the records you generate that apply to your personnel, such as your employee handbook or other general information or policies that you provide to each employee. Permanently retain any policies you create independently for your business. However, when dealing with policy information from outside agencies and authorities, we suggest keeping the information until it is updated or replaced.

Employee Handbook	*Until superseded or updated, then transfer to Permanent Files*
General Information/Policies	*Current year plus one; selectively retain*

Benefits

Keep here the records associated with the administration of the employment benefits that you provide for your employees. Subdivide this section by the types of benefits extended, for example, health insurance, life insurance, accident insurance, workers' compensation. Keep records of remittances to the insuring company with your financial files ("Accounts Payable") and employee benefit payments with employee payroll records, also in the financial files ("Salaries and Wages").

Benefit #1:	General Correspondence	*Current year plus one, then destroy*
	Policy and Agreements	*Until expired*
	Claims (by employee name)	*Until settled and all limitation periods have expired*
Benefit #2:	General Correspondence	*Current year plus one, then destroy*
	Policy and Agreements	*Until expired*
	Claims (by employee name)	*Until settled and all limitation periods have expired*

Most benefit records fall into three subcategories:

- routine correspondence, which has little ongoing value
- the policy or agreement documents, which are valuable for as long as you hold the policies
- claims that might be made for the benefits

When claims are made against benefit coverage, the records may become the property of the insurance carrier, or the office of primary responsibility may move from you to the carrier or claims adjuster. It's a good idea to keep all records associated with any claim, unless you are specifically advised otherwise by your insurance company or legal advisor. Note: each employee's file will also have the particular benefits that the employee is entitled to or receives.

Contractors and Subcontractors

Keep here records associated with contractors, subcontractors or consultants that you engage to do project work for your company. (Again, any financial statements and receipts associated with services received or work completed will be filed in the "Accounts Payable" category.)

Contractor (by name of person or company)	*Until project over or contract fulfilled and all outstanding issues settled; store for one more year, then destroy*

Employees

Keep here records associated with your employees, both general information that applies to all employees (notices of holidays, office hours and so on), and individual employee files, in which the records of each employee are kept. Depending upon the size or complexity of your business, employee records might include such documents as employees' résumés, applications, offers of appointment, awards, training records and certificates. All individual employee records should be classified as confidential, with limited access to the files by other company employees.

Employees—General	*Current year plus one, then destroy*
Employees (alphabetical by last name)	*Until employment ceases, then store until all regulatory obligations have expired*

Tip: Keep Your File Size Manageable

Employment periods may be for a very long time, and it is possible for an employee file to grow to an inconvenient size. If you want to divide the employee file into a more manageable size, close off the current file, attaching a note indicating the file continues as a second volume. Create a new file folder (labelled by name, Volume 2) to continue collecting employee information. Move the older file to storage, where it is still accessible if you need it but not in the way. You might want to apply this tip to other unwieldy files.

Health and Safety

Keep here records relating to regulations about workplace safety, correspondence with regulatory authorities governing workplace safety, and workers' compensation coverages your business requires. This category includes routine correspondence as well as information circulars and instructions from regulatory bodies.

Depending upon where you live, this category will

include information about mandatory or optional workers' safety program coverage, such as Workers' Compensation in Canada or the Occupational Safety and Health Administration (OSHA) in the United States, to which your company contributes. While this is a form of insurance, you likely will want to keep all safety-related information here rather than in "Insurance." Keep the financial documents for remittance with your financial records, in "Accounts Payable."

This category also includes information on accidents and injuries suffered by your employees on the job and any information about health or safety programs you provide or facilitate for your employees. Depending upon the industry in which your business operates, these records may have a very long retention requirement. For example, if an employee is in an accident involving toxic chemicals, you might have to keep information on the accident even beyond the lifetime of the employee. Again, we caution you to be aware of the regulatory and legal obligations upon your company. Safety training materials should be filed with other training records (under "Training"). Individual employee ratings, certifications or qualifications are filed in each employee's file.

General Correspondence	*Current year plus one, then destroy*
Circulars, Directives and Orders	*Until updated or replaced*
Coverage (by regulatory body)	*Until updated or coverage ceases*
Accidents and Injuries (by employee name or event)	*Until all claims are completed and records are no longer required for legal purposes*

Hiring and Recruitment

Keep here records about your hiring procedures, advertisements for positions, and correspondence with headhunters or employment agencies. Also keep here any résumés or inquiries about employment that you receive. You may have a practice of keeping résumés on file for a period of time, to fill vacancies as they arise. Keep in mind that résumés become dated, so although it is useful to have them on file for reference, the longer you keep them, the less helpful they may be to your future personnel needs. The résumé of a successful applicant should be filed in the employee's individual file. You might want to selectively retain competition advertisements and descriptions for future reference.

General Correspondence	*Current year plus one, then destroy*
Hiring Competitions (by job title, date)	*Current year plus one; selectively retain*
Hiring Procedures	*Until updated or replaced*
Résumés (unsolicited)	*Keep for one year, then destroy*

Training

Keep here the materials associated with current training, professional development or continuing education programs. These may be sessions or courses that you offer to your employees in-house, that you sponsor your employees to attend or that your employees are obliged to undertake to obtain qualifications or certification. If you offer an in-house event or course, file here the planning, arrangements and program offering, including room bookings, registrations, speakers and so on. You will probably want to selectively retain information giving the program title, date and speaker name in the Permanent Files to document company history and for interest. Bills and financial records are kept in "Accounts Payable," and employee certificates or participation documents are filed in the individual employee files. Upon completion of activities, keep the training materials, books, manuals or other publications in a reference file, reference library or on your bookshelf.

Company-Offered Programs (by name, date)	*Current year plus one; selectively retain in Permanent Files*
Company-Supported Programs	*Current only, then discard*

Premises

Records in this section relate to the premises your business occupies. For some businesses, this is a workspace in the home. Maybe it's the garage. For others it is an office space, an industrial space, a studio or workshop, a plant or a distribution facility that the business owns or leases.

If you are working at home, this section may consist of one file folder containing information about the way in which you split costs between your office and your household. On the other hand, if you operate in a separate business location, you will require separate files or subdivisions of information to accommodate the complexity of your arrangements. As previously discussed, any financial records associated with your premises, such as receipts or invoices, will always be filed with your financial records, in "Accounts Payable" files.

Lease

Keep here the lease and any other related correspondence associated with premises that you lease to operate your business. If you feel more comfortable keeping the signed lease agreement off-site or in a safety deposit box, then keep a photocopy here for reference. If, as part of your business operation, you lease space to others, then file the leases with the operational files under "Customers/Clients."

Correspondence	*Current year plus one; destroy when lease has expired or been updated and any outstanding issues are resolved*
Lease Agreement	*Until expired or updated, then transfer to storage and retain until all legal obligations have passed*

Maintenance

Keep here any records relating to premises maintenance. These include agreements and correspondence about cleaning services, repairs or other maintenance requirements. Invoices from the services and receipts for payments will be retained with the financial files, in "Accounts Payable."

Cleaning Service	*Until contract expired and all outstanding issues resolved*
Repair Service	*Until contract expired and all outstanding issues resolved*

Utilities

Keep here correspondence, licences and other papers related to office utilities such as heat, light, telecommunications and so on. Reminder: file your receipts and invoices in your financial files, in "Accounts Payable."

Cable		*Current year plus one, then transfer to storage and retain until no longer required for audit or taxation purposes*
Electricity		*Current year plus one, then transfer to storage and retain until no longer required for audit or taxation purposes*
Gas (Natural/Propane)		*Current year plus one, then transfer to storage and retain until no longer required for audit or taxation purposes*
Internet Service Provider		*Current year plus one, then transfer to storage and retain until no longer required for audit or taxation purposes*
Telephone:	Cellular	*Current year plus one, then transfer to storage and retain until no longer required for audit or taxation purposes*
	Local	*Current year plus one, then transfer to storage and retain until no longer required for audit or taxation purposes*
	Long Distance	*Current year plus one, then transfer to storage and retain until no longer required for audit or taxation purposes*
Water and Sewer		*Current year plus one, then transfer to storage and retain until no longer required for audit or taxation purposes*

Operational Files

Just to refresh your memory, unlike the administrative files we've just been discussing, which are fairly standard for most businesses, operational files are unique and related to your specific business. These are diverse record types that may or may not have regulatory requirements. However, these records will have operating value to the business and may in fact have long-term retention requirements. Examples include:

Business Plan

Keep here your current and past business plans, your ideas and dreams, your financial projections and any other information that helps you organize, direct and make future plans for your business. Keep here any advice you receive from external advisors on all aspects of your business operation.

Advisors	*Keep current advice/reports, then transfer to Permanent Files*
Financial Plan	*Current and previous versions, then transfer to Permanent Files*
Operational Plan	*Current and previous versions, then transfer to Permanent Files*

Tip: Let Your Reference Files Work for You

Don't forget to use your Reference Files as a source of inspiration and ideas that you can incorporate into your business planning. Use those sample formats you've been saving to design your website. Fine-tune your corporate image by incorporating ideas from favourite brochures.

Customers/Clients

Without customers and clients, you wouldn't have a business. Treat these records with the same respect you accord your customers. You should consider these a vital record series, and so, in addition to filing for daily work, consider how else you might want to protect them. (You might want to duplicate them, store them in a separate location or back up a computer file, for example.) Various types of security are discussed in chapter 6.

Depending upon the nature of your business, there may be regulations affecting how you maintain, access and store your client files. For example, health care providers must follow certain regulations governing the privacy of client files. Know what your responsibilities are and develop your record-keeping practices accordingly.

When you have an ongoing relationship with a client, you might find it more convenient to file by customer name and year, then keep files from past years in storage. You might still need to refer to the earlier documents, but your main interactions will be documented in the recent files.

Customers/Clients (alphabetical by name)	*Current year, then transfer to storage; retain until end of relationship and until all legal obligations have passed*

Inventory

Keep here records relating to the ordering, tracking and dispersal of the inventory of products you sell. If you are a craft business owner, this is where you would keep track of all your items for sale. Remember, inventory control is not just what products go out, it is also what materials come in. If you are assembling a craft or product, your inventory files will include lists of source materials as well as lists of your finished product. If you are using a computer application to track and manage your inventory, then file only your paper correspondence about inventory in this section. Whether the records are paper or electronic, you need to decide on retention guidelines, then follow them.

Inventory—Raw Material	*Current year plus one, then transfer to storage and retain until no longer required for audit or taxation purposes*
Inventory—Finished Products	*Current year plus one, then transfer to storage and retain until no longer required for audit or taxation purposes*

Marketing

Keep here records associated with marketing functions, strategies and activities in your company, including your market surveys, sales projections, sales territories, sales organization, sales promotions and campaigns, advertising blitzes and so on. If yours is a sales-oriented organization, these records are also vital to your company. You might link sales records to customer files ("Customers/Clients") or financial files ("Accounts Receivable"), but the records kept here document the advertising, marketing and sales activities of you and your staff. The actual sales records of products sold will be filed in the "Product Sales" category.

Advertising	*Current year plus one, then transfer to Permanent Files*
Marketing Plan	*Until updated, then transfer to Permanent Files*
Sales Campaigns and Promotions (subdivide by campaign name)	*Until complete, then transfer to Permanent Files*
Sales Organization and Territories	*Until updated; selectively retain*

Presentations and Seminars

Keep here records related to formal presentations, seminars or workshops that you or your employees give to others—customers, prospective customers, for public relations or any other purpose. For each presentation, save the speakers' notes or speeches and lists of (or references to) any audiovisual materials used (photographs, overheads, computer presentation disks and so on, which may have to be filed elsewhere because of their format or large size). Note: the difference between this category and "Conferences and Conventions" in the Reference Files is that this category reflects presentations, seminars and workshops you give (your intellectual property), rather than notes or information collected from presentations you attend.

Presentations (alphabetical by title and date)	*Current year plus one,* *then transfer to Permanent Files*

Tip: Track Those Talks

If you do a lot of presentations, consider keeping a summary list of them on paper or in a database. This list will be filed in your Business Files (under "Presentations and Seminars"). It will help you keep track of when, where and to whom you spoke over the years, plus it will help you to locate specific notes or all-important lists of attendees that may have gone to your Permanent Files. Use this as an idea generator for future talks.

Product Sales

Keep here records associated with your sales. If you are using a computer application to track results and manage your sales, then file only your paper correspondence here.

Sales (by sales period)	*Current year plus one, then transfer to storage and retain until no longer required for audit or taxation purposes*

Projects

As with the customer/client files, project files may represent the reason your company is in business. For example, a consulting firm will have a file for each project to identify the proposed and actual work undertaken for the client. Depending upon the project, a project file might be arranged in date order from start to finish, or it might be subdivided into standard functions within the project, for example "Project X—Proposal"; "Project X—Background and Supporting Documentation"; "Project X—Meetings"; "Project X—Schedule"; "Project X—Reports and Recommendations."

Projects (alphabetical by project name or client)	*Until project over and all outstanding issues settled, then transfer to Permanent Files*
Proposals	*Current year plus one*

You may want to have a file folder labelled "Proposals" for holding any proposal until the work is secured. Once an agreement for the work is signed, move the proposal to your project series files. Keep your outstanding proposals for the current year plus one (or whatever time frame is reasonable in your line of business). If the project comes back to life after this time, you'll likely want to rewrite the proposal anyway.

Tip: Distinguish Clients and Projects	What is the difference between a client and a project? The client hired you to perform a project. A client will hire you again to conduct another project. Same client—different project. Avoid client/project confusion by filing projects separately in the "Projects" category.

Supplies

Keep here the records and correspondence associated with your company's suppliers. This also includes the latest product catalogues and price lists for the items that you use in your operations. Remember that the administrative category *Equipment, Supplies and Services* is already in place for the routine supplies that you require as a business. In this section you would file information about the supplies and suppliers specifically associated with your particular business purpose. For example, if you operate a landscaping service, in this section you would keep track of the companies that provide you with the plants, soil materials and special equipment you need to operate your business.

Suppliers (alphabetical by name)	*Until end of relationship, then transfer to storage until all legal requirements have passed*

Reminder: these proposed operational files are examples only to show you how to determine what your operational files will be. Study your business functions and establish your operational files according to these functions. Don't fret if your categories do not match those we have suggested. You may not need them all.

Permanent Files

With regard to records, "permanent" can and does mean a variety of things—everything from "keep forever" to "keep for the life of the company" to "keep until all legal obligations have been fulfilled." The reason you develop a permanent records section is because you will not be disposing of these records for a very long time, if at all, and you want to minimize the time you spend handling these files. Legal obligations may extend over a very long period of time. Free up some extra space and save yourself a lot of unnecessary paper handling by putting here documents that you don't need to regularly access or reference. Once a year, when you go through your files during an annual purge or review (see page 111), check to confirm the need to continue housing these records.

You may need or want to keep information in this category for practical (perhaps legal or reference) reasons or impractical (for instance, sentimental) reasons. Compared to the volume and number of files in the other categories, there is typically a lot less information in this category. The main feature of this type of record is that it has value for the entire life of your business. Some records may have to be kept to satisfy regulatory requirements even after your business operations have ceased.

A key point: permanent records are not destroyed. Do you recall the information life cycle that we discussed earlier? Records are created or received, used, filed for reference, and then, in most cases, destroyed—with the exception being those records you have identified as permanent. Some files will indeed travel through the filing system from Fingertip to Business to Permanent Files, while others, such as an incorporation document, may be placed immediately into the Permanent Files.

Permanent documents require special care. You are keeping this information because it documents the history of your business or you are required by law to keep it for a long period of time. Consequently, these records should be placed into files and containers that are intended to protect and conserve them. You may want to consider acid-free folders or other archival-quality containers (such as photo albums) to house long-term paper records, or you may require a fireproof container to house vital paper and electronic records. These housing devices cost more than conventional filing materials and supplies but will extend the lifetime and protect the condition of your records.

Agreements/Contracts

Keep here any original, signed agreements between your company and others. Working copies of agreements can and should be readily available in the Business Files. Arrange agreements or contracts by name of the other party.

Agreement #1	*Until expired and all outstanding legal obligations are fulfilled*

Tip: Manage Your Contracts	Protect your company's interests by setting up a register to track every contract or agreement you sign. Jot down what the contract covers, its duration and when it expires. Treat the list as a vital record.

Financial Documents

Keep here your financial statements and the annual summary of your general ledger (which may be a legal requirement in your jurisdiction).

Annual Summary	*Until company ceases to exist and all legal obligations are fulfilled*
Financial Statements	*Until company ceases to exist and all legal obligations are fulfilled*

Incorporation/Registration Documents

Keep here the legal incorporation, partnership or registration documents that establish your company or business entity.

Incorporation/Registration Documents	*Until company ceases to exist and all legal obligations are fulfilled*

Your business may begin informally and evolve into a corporate or legal entity. Keeping the chain of documents intact will be, in this case, important for historic and reference purposes. When the small photography business, Sam's Photos, becomes a leading photo franchise, Sam's Photos Inc., the documents of its early years take on valuable historic perspective. So don't throw Permanent Files out.

Minutes

Keep here the minutes and agendas of significant meetings. For many types of organizations, minutes include key resolutions, decisions and policies directing the business. Consequently, minutes are valuable for future reference. You may be obliged to retain the minutes of the company's annual meeting or you may be obliged to submit an annual report to a regulatory body. It is more useful than obligatory to keep internal minutes, since they detail the company's decision-making and history.

Annual Reports	*Retain permanently*
Minutes (by committee name and date)	*Retain permanently*

Photographs and Graphic Material

Keep here photographs and graphic material that document the history of your business. Photographic and graphic material (including negatives) requires special care to preserve and protect it, such as archival-quality envelopes, albums and storage boxes.

If you are Sam of Sam's Photos, then photos are, of course, your product. The photos we are talking about here are those that document the growth and history of your business (such as photos of the first storefront, from public events or from staff parties). Note: photographs may be found in other filing categories, but it's a good idea to consolidate the best ones here to simplify the process of caring for them properly.

Photographs (by date or subject)	*Retain permanently*
Graphic Material (by subject)	*Retain permanently*

Project, Sales or Activity Files

Keep here operational records (for example, projects, photo shoots, consulting studies, awards and honours) that you have decided to selectively retain permanently to document the history and development of your business. Think "company archives" when you are selecting the records here. The documents here are the ones you have chosen to selectively retain permanently from the operational records in the Business Files.

Projects	*Retain permanently*
Sales	*Retain permanently*
Activities	*Retain permanently*

Publications

Keep here in-house newsletters, booklets, brochures, press releases and other publications that you or your staff have produced. Keep manuscript as well as setup material, graphics, photographs and other original material you have commissioned for inclusion in your publications.

Publications (by title and date)	*Retain permanently*

Reference Files

We like this category! We like it because we know it will take care of a lot of paper clutter scattered around the office. The information contained here is of interest to you but is not created by you and is not crucial to the operation of your business. The reasons for keeping information here are because you think you might refer to it again or it is background information to provide ideas, inspiration or general business intelligence.

Information kept here is transitory. It is passing through the organization, making a brief stop in the files because you think you might use it sometime in the near future.

We would expect the Reference Files for a sales-oriented organization to include information about competitors, the general sales environment in which the business operates and business trends. On the other hand, for a freelance writer, these files might include sample articles, background information for potential stories and an ideas file. These files should contain the "interesting" information that business professionals tend to collect and which, if uncontrolled, tends to accumulate in (read "clutter up") the other office files.

You might find that information kept here is a source of ideas and inspiration for your business planning. However, in the end, most of what you keep here is time-sensitive and can become outdated quickly. A good rule of thumb to use with this class of information is to discard a document if you haven't referred to it within two years. We want you to be ruthless here, because this area is a potential mess. You will need to regularly remove and purge the records. File information here, regardless of format, by meaningful topic or subject. Categories might include:

Books and Book Lists	*Current year plus previous*
Business Trends (electronic commerce, Internet connectivity)	*Current year only*
Competitors	*Current year plus previous*
Conferences and Conventions (including notes and handouts from those attended)	*Current year plus previous*
Course Offerings	*Current year only*
Industry Trends and News	*Current year only*
Travel Information (maps, guidebooks)	*Current only, until updated*

Information on business and industry trends might be useful for your business planning and contribute to business intelligence. Consequently, you might move this information into your Business Files if it becomes part of your business planning.

Reference information rapidly becomes dated. Get to know your local library, and be prepared to conduct research when you need to know current information or want to develop ideas and strategies. Don't waste too much time clipping magazines, bookmarking websites and maintaining files of interest to you; your time is too valuable, and your local library may have access to current print and electronic resources. Most larger libraries have clipping files or access to electronic databases that include full-text newspaper articles.

Tip: Hire an Information Specialist

Save time. Let a trained information specialist be your guide to reference information sources. These experts can quickly locate accurate and reliable information from on-line as well as print sources, which is well worth the money. Look in the yellow pages of your telephone directory under headings such as "Information Services" or check with your local library association.

4
What About Electronic Records?

Managing Digital Information

DO YOU USE A COMPUTER IN YOUR BUSINESS? IF YOU DON'T, YOU may skip this chapter. If you do, read on. Business communication and transactions produce information in a number of formats, including paper, digital, photographic and other records. We focus in this chapter on computer-generated information (also referred to as digital or electronic information), because its management brings some special challenges.

When you think about it, how you deal with your electronic files or faxes should be no different than the way you cope with paperwork. By *electronic records,* we mean the information you create or receive on your computer or internal fax, including text, data and image files, electronic mail, faxes and information downloaded from the Internet. Format doesn't matter as much as subject or function. Regardless of format, later on you will want to find these individual files.

Just like us, you have probably heard it said—and are still hearing—that the computer will replace paper in business, that the future is digital, not paper based. Should you believe it? Maybe the question should be rephrased. Does anybody think about it any more? It seems a lot of people are pretty busy printing out information from electronic sources onto paper. Consider the amount of information you receive digitally but end up printing out for ease-of-reading or reference purposes.

This ranges from e-mails to in-house documents and reports, Web-based information from full-text databases, government documents made available in pdf format, forms, information about products and services from websites, interesting words of wisdom from personal websites, and more.

The computer can be a wonderful ally and support to businesses, or it can be an enemy. Which role it plays depends upon your wisdom, common sense and, in some cases, patience as you embrace the digital age, with all its promise and capability. Here's what we've learned (sometimes the hard way!) about managing electronic records, along with some tips and advice.

The blessing of computer technology is that with the right software applications for your business, your personal and corporate productivity can increase dramatically. Using databases to collect, calculate and keep track of transactions, customers, inventory and projects can save time and increase staff productivity and service. Electronic mail enables you to communicate around the world, independent of the clock, to maintain contact, promote your products or sell your services. If you are away from the office, with the right software and communications system you can operate your business as if you were there. Electronic commerce is promising to transform the ways in which business is conducted. The list of advantages goes on. Our purpose here is to help you manage the records that result from the computer systems you use.

The curse of computer technology is that you can easily lose valuable information on the computer. Losses occur either accidentally through a system crash or failure, through the obsolescence of systems and software, and by simply misfiling it. Have you ever saved information on disk, then left the disks overnight in the car, only to have them be unreadable the next day? Have you upgraded a software program, then discovered that you can no longer access saved file information? Or have you selected a software program that disappears from the market, leaving you with no upgrading capability or technical support (what's known as an *orphan system*) or, worse, no compatibility with other systems?

When you are working with computer records, you need a coherent technology plan, appropriate training and a comprehensive record-keeping strategy. Regarding the latter, you need to organize your strategy, go forward with a plan and be aware of the record-keeping issues that you face. Elements of such a plan include methods for naming electronic files, protecting electronic formats and insuring your records against technological obsolescence.

Naming Files and Directories

First of all, let's get the terms straight. We want to define what we mean by a *record* in the computer environment. When using a computer, you name your documents, usually according to a naming convention that the software will permit. A single computer document is usually called a *file*. You will create and save a number of related computer files in a *folder*. The folders are usually arrayed in a *directory,* which is a larger folder, similar to a file drawer. The most important rule with computer records in this type of setup is to be consistent with what you name your files, folders and directories.

From our discussion of paper records in chapter 2, the logic behind category and file names is that they are based on the subject of the documents and the relationship between documents. The same principle applies here: name your individual files with a meaningful subject or title that will help you find the file easily later on, when it is not so fresh in your mind. You will find computer documents more readily if you have been consistent in naming them and saving them in an appropriate place.

In the recent past, most software programs limited the size of the name you could apply, which sometimes made it hard to give files a meaningful name. Some companies used codes, rather than names or subjects, to fit a title into the limited space available. You may still be working with software that has this built-in limitation. However, most programs now have sufficient space to allow you to use the exact title or subject you want, written out in full. This capability makes the file-naming task much easier.

With each type of software (word-processing, spreadsheet, database, graphics), you create single documents, or files, usually related to subjects or functions. It makes sense, then, to use the same names for computer directories that you use for your paper file categories.

Within each software application, create a directory system and divide it into the four broad categories: Fingertip, Business, Permanent and Reference. Go down one level within each of these and create folders for each of the file names that you have already assigned to your paper files. Then create a meaningful name for individual documents. Place them within these folders. The use of these electronic files and their organizational logic will be the same as for the paper documents.

Whether your records are paper or electronic, always use the same logic and filing structure as outlined in chapter 2. In fact, use exactly the same file plan, list your files exactly the same way, and keep a master list of files that includes all files, regardless of format (paper, digital, photographic, etc.). Simply put an asterisk or notation on the master list to indicate which files or folders are located on the computer hard drive rather than in the filing cabinet. Your paper file may have an electronic component, or your electronic file may have some matching paper correspondence in a file folder. For example, your invoices may be in electronic files in your accounting system, while your paper file includes the customer's correspondence and payment information to you. The format of the record doesn't matter. Your master filing plan will help you locate the information regardless of location.

Tip: Persistence Pays Off

You've heard it before—21 days to a new habit. So stick with your new procedures for managing information. Discipline yourself. If you follow the outline we have suggested, you will soon find it second nature to name files according to your new file plan.

Protecting Your Computer Information

After determining how to name your files, the next pressing issue is how to protect the information from accidental loss. Information in the electronic domain is fragile, subject to loss due to a careless keystroke, a power surge or a power failure. Several years of valuable information can be gone in seconds. Or your office could be robbed, and although the loss of computer hardware is serious, the loss of data on your computer can finish your business. Therefore, it's important to develop a regular backup plan and then implement it. It's likely that your computer trainers, books or manuals told you to back up your data. But we all look for short-cuts or time-savers when we're busy. Skipping over this step can be a costly mistake. A regular backup of all your data is critical.

How often should you back up your data? Frequency will depend upon your business cycle. Ask yourself "How long will it take me to re-create my records if they are lost?" If the answer is "longer than I have time for," then make this backup a priority. Some information may be irreplaceable. Most organizations routinely complete a series of partial backups and do a full backup less frequently. You will know best the right time to conduct a full or partial backup of your data. We suggest that the backup cycle mirror your regular computerwork activities Daily may be too often, but probably at least once a week is good practice

For security's sake, keep your backup data in a safe place some distance away from your computer. Some small-business operators take a copy to their bank safety deposit box. Others simply take it home or away from their business premises. Don't keep it in your car. Fluctuations in temperature may cause your data to disappear. All this applies to data from laptops, too. In addition, laptops are more susceptible to loss and theft than wired-in office machines.

Guarding against Obsolescence

In the rapidly changing digital domain, nothing seems to change more often than software. There are new program releases, version upgrades, rewrites, superseded programs. Adapting to new software means that you have to keep your data current or synchronized with the version of software you are using. Why? Because if you don't bring even your two-year-old files forward each time you upgrade the software, you may be unable to read, and consequently to use, these older files. If the electronic copy is your only copy of your older records, you may find that you have no information, because it is inaccessible to you. Large corporations are now investing in software dedicated to maintaining digital information in a current state.

Not only software, but also hardware and storage devices rapidly become obsolete. It wasn't that long ago that 5¼-inch floppy disks became 3½-inch floppies, which are now probably on their way to being replaced by compact disks and digital audiotape. If you use any kind of computer, you have to keep up to date with the changes that are constantly occurring and know how they will affect you and your ability to retrieve and use your computerized business information.

Tip: Consider Paper Copies

If your business depends upon electronic information being accessible over time and you want to retain a permanent or archival copy, consider generating a paper copy of your digital records and filing them with your paper files for safekeeping. Print out the full e-mail message, including attachments or other threads related to the original message. When in doubt, paper copies win out!

Keeping the Whole Record

When you receive a letter or other paper document, you are able to discern the meaning of the record not only by what the message says, but also by who sent it on what date, and you can attribute importance to the record by the signature and other elements. This extra information is known as *metadata,* or data about the data. Electronic records also contain metadata. If you consider electronic mail, for example, to interpret it you need to know not only what the message says, but also the header information—the date and time, who sent the message, by what system and so on. You may also need to access the documents attached to the e-mail message in order to receive and understand the full communication.

The point here is that you should save not only the content of your electronic messages, but also the metadata, in order to provide meaning and context to fully understand the messages later. You will also need the system software and system hardware to read the record, and the actual message conveyed by or saved from the system. Sure is a lot more complicated than the paper documents in a file folder stored in a filing cabinet, read by human eyes.

Managing Scanned Records

With the increasing storage power available, some businesses are actively scanning or creating a digital copy of all incoming paper records. It is possible to store information in an exclusively digital environment. Low-cost, high-resolution scanners are now available, and the input of information is as easy as making a photocopy. As long as you are aware of the pros and cons of storing your information in a computerized environment, an all-digital environment may be a suitable option. Be aware that scanned records, in order to be found again, will require the same type of directory or file-naming conventions we described earlier.

New business practices are arising, with service bureaus advertising that they will convert your paper records to digital format. Other firms advertise that you can send or upload your scanned digital records off-site, store them in a remote computer, then access and retrieve them from your desktop as you need them. So, yes, the "less paper"(versus paperless) office is achievable. But we'll never be persuaded that paper will disappear altogether.

Storing Records Off-Site

As with paper records, inactive electronic records can be sent off-site. There are commercial services now that advertise vaulting and archiving services. In other words, these companies will accept, store and return to your office your digital files, following the same principles as the agencies that store and retrieve boxes of paper records. The details of the storage process will depend upon the service agency you select. However, when your records are all in digital format, it is relatively simple to transmit them to an off-site location via a telecommunications network. You can sleep at night knowing your records are secure.

Electronic Mail

Records management experts have described electronic mail as the most important record type to manage in the computerized office. We create or receive electronic messages even more frequently than we do conventional messages. In some businesses, exchange of information is done exclusively via electronic mail.

E-mail messages consist of several parts. In addition to the message body, the e-mail also includes (in the header) data about who sent the message, when, at what time, and it may also include attachments. The entire three-part message may have value to your business. Consequently, e-mail messages received are as important as your internally generated electronic records.

Remember, we discussed unsorted e-mail when we reviewed a computerwork coping strategy in chapter 2. Don't make the mistake of filing e-mail in an unsorted gigantic "e-mail file," because it will be too large to facilitate finding messages later. Depending upon the software you use, you should establish an in-basket, then electronically file the messages to the same four categories already discussed: Fingertip, Business, Permanent and Reference. Further subdivide each category as you need, according to your master file plan. You probably don't have to be as detailed as with your paper file categories, but you will likely still need subdivisions for individual projects or clients within your Business Files. The nature of your business will govern how detailed your categories need to be.

One consideration with e-mail messages is to determine where you want to keep an official record of an e-mail transaction or transmittal. Depending upon the importance of the message, you might want to print out the message and attachment, then file the hard copies in your paper files. The printed record will include all three elements of the e-mail message. Good housekeeping practice means that you should also delete the electronic message from your computer when the paper copy is your official record.

How Long Should You Keep It?

It's wise to give some thought to the retention of electronic messages, since your directory of e-mail messages will grow rapidly. It is the content of the message, rather than the medium, that governs how long you will keep it. For example, if you undertake electronic commerce, some of your e-mail messages may be part of your financial records or your operational records. Therefore, you need to follow the retention guidelines that you have established for that record grouping. You will have other e-mail messages (including junk e-mail) that are routine messages that can be read and discarded immediately.

Tip: Don't Waste Time on Junk E-Mail

Some experts suggest that you not respond at all to junk e-mail. However, if it is your practice to respond, have a prepared message to automatically send back to any message you consider to be "junk" e-mail. In addition, take advantage of a service to have your e-mail information added to an "opt-out" list circulated to various direct-marketing association members at www.e-mps.org. Take the same care with your e-mail address that you take with your personal and business addresses.

Faxes

Your computer system may have the capability of sending and receiving faxes. Faxes are another type of electronic record that may be received and stored electronically or in paper form. Apply to faxes the same principles as you apply to your electronic mail. Remember that each fax message is actually a two-part message: the information that is transmitted or received, and the information about the transmission or receipt, including who sent it, when and at what time. You may want to print out your transmission log regularly if you use the fax system to transmit or receive time-sensitive materials, such as bids or prices. Again, the nature of your business will govern how important this "extra" information (the transmission log) will be.

An example of the importance of the transmission log occurred when an agency submitted a request for funds to a government department. The receiving fax machine was out of order and the agency was informed that it had missed the deadline. However, by producing a transmission log, agency staff proved that the submission had indeed been sent in time, and government funds were provided.

Tip: Retention Guidelines	Apply your retention schedule equally to records in all formats, including e-mail and all files in computer directories. Remember, you don't have to keep everything forever.

The Internet

Oh, what a tangled Web we've woven! The Internet, with the World Wide Web, has opened up all sorts of possibilities for businesses, from high-speed, global communication to e-commerce transactions to quick and easy dissemination of information. Never before have small businesses been able to develop a customer base, establish a profile, conduct business or access information with such ease. There is a lot of information about the Internet out there. Sources range from your know-it-all neighbour to magazine and newspaper articles, courses and computer-dedicated TV programs. Here we raise some of the Internet issues that relate to information management.

Before getting carried away with ideas about the possibilities for your business with the Internet or the World Wide Web, you should consider the importance of protecting your information. With an Internet connection, your information and ideas may be accessible to the casual or dedicated hacker. Your Internet connection may be providing an unlocked entrance into your computer, where the information can be corrupted or stolen. So you need to adopt a defensive strategy, which likely would include a firewall. A *firewall*, just as it sounds, is a device that prevents unauthorized access to your computer or system. Talk to your local Internet service provider or technical support person, who should be able to tell you what solutions are best for you.

You also need to protect your information from viruses. You will want to run a program that can scan for viruses before you download anything from outside sources. This scan can detect any virus or unsafe condition that could compromise or damage your system.

When searching the Web for information, ask yourself "How reliable or authentic is this information?" Anyone can post information to a website. You may determine that this information is useful to you. But how do you know how accurate it is? Who put it up there? Are the sources real, reliable, authentic? When you read a conventional book, a newspaper or information from another source, you obtain clues about the value of the information by knowing who wrote it, who published it, what authority is behind it and so on. On a website, look for ownership information, contact information and the date the site was last updated before deciding upon the legitimacy of the information.

Managing Records from Your Corporate Website

You may decide to establish a corporate website as part of your business operations. When you consider the factors involved (the subject of many other books and reference guides), consider also the record-keeping implications associated with your site.

How will you document what you put on the site? For some businesses, their website is a place to post newsletters, news releases, product descriptions and similar material. If this describes your website, a dated copy of the content of the Web pages will provide an adequate record of what is mounted and maintained. In other words, take periodic "snapshots" of the information, so that a future record is available for your business purposes.

If you are setting up an interactive website, with functions for customers to ask questions, receive answers, place orders and conduct other business with your company, then you will require some specific processes for collecting and saving transactional information from the website.

These requirements for saving information, similar to your requirements for saving accounting invoices in the paper world, provide your business with documentation to coordinate your transactions or later provide proof of activities. These requirements for saving and tracking transactions are part of the specifications you should develop for your website design. Provide these requirements to the systems people and ensure that some method is put in place to collect your information.

How much you use a computer will ultimately depend upon the nature of your business and your own technology comfort level. Don't overlook the potential benefits of computer applications. But recognize that computers will produce records that, like the paper ones you know and deal with, will require care and preservation for future reference.

5
How to Keep It?

Maintaining Your Office Filing System

NOW THAT YOU'VE TAKEN THE TIME TO SET UP THE LOGICAL categories for your records, how do you set up the physical folders in your office? We recommend that you use readily available file folders and labels from your local stationery shop. It is quite simple and painless to set up a filing system and then keep it maintained, provided you establish a maintenance routine. Experts say it takes about 21 days of practising a new activity before that activity becomes an ingrained habit or routine. So give yourself a month of managing your paperwork according to your plan to ensure the maintenance process becomes part of your business routine.

Let's take a look at three facets of file maintenance:

- the daily requirements for keeping the incoming and outgoing information under control
- the less frequent (perhaps monthly) overview, during which you check your categories for ongoing relevance, make new ones, update databases and conduct other management activities
- the annual purge or cleanout, in which you toss, shred or remove to off-site storage the records whose use has ended. This is also when you move your electronic files to your designated storage space if you haven't already done that.

With an information management system in place, each one of these activities should take very little of your precious time—unlike before, when paper accumulations were a regular stressor for you.

Daily Routine

The most pressing regular task you or someone in your office has to perform is to receive incoming information—mail, faxes, e-mail, couriered parcels—and ensure that it is processed into the appropriate files.

Processing this information on a daily basis should be a priority for most offices. The "action" in the office is all based on current information—the latest quotes, the most recent invoices and so on. If the current information is not handled immediately but piles up, pretty soon you will face the same problems that caused you to buy this book. Realistically, if you don't have time to do this on a daily basis, make sure that at least three times per week you attend to incoming information as follows:

- Establish a place to put the information—an "in-basket" or similar place—until you can attend to it.
- Open the mail and quickly review each item, sorting it into your four categories: Fingertip, Business, Permanent and Reference.
- Take each category in turn, beginning with the Fingertip Files. Sort the information into your established subcategories, and place it in your filing device according to the category or date of action.
- For information that is to go into the Business, Reference and Permanent Files, simply write the filing category and

subcategory in pencil on each document, sort them into alphabetical order, and file them into the appropriate file folders (If you have to create new file folders, save the process of formal labelling and list updating for your monthly routine.)

- Remember to take care of your electronic mail. Sort out your messages in a timely fashion.

For now, you've put away the information and can find it when you need it.

Monthly Routine

Set aside some time once a month to type up new folder labels, revise your file list, check your categories and perform other file maintenance. You can take a little more time with your filing system at this point to decide what is working or not and adjust categories if changes should be made. If you've been keeping up your daily routine, you won't be pressured by piles of unprocessed papers!

When you create new folders, design labels using the label-making function in your computer software. Check to see what preformatted label brands and sizes are compatible. Pick a label size that gives you enough room to type a readable subject or file title.

Labelling is important, whether it is for a file folder, computer disk, binder, basket or tote box, to identify the contents of the container. It may seem unnecessary at first, especially if you have few records to manage, but very quickly you will forget where you have placed records, and the lack of a label will cost you time. You don't have to invest in any special labelling devices, because most recent word-processing software programs have preformatted label-making functions. You can select the label manufacturer and label size to prepare typed labels not only for file folders but also for other media formats, such as videos and computer disks. If you find it too cumbersome to make computer-generated labels, stick to handwritten labels. Functionality should win out over aesthetics. We emphasize the importance here of labelling your computer disks. As removable media, they are useless to you without any indication of software and date of file stored.

Update your file list by printing off a new listing of all your files. Make this list the first item in your filing cabinet. Locate other copies where you need them.

We recommend that you implement a colour coding system. Colour helps your eye to place or find information intuitively and quickly. You can use colour any way you choose, but typically people select a coloured label or a coloured file folder. Depending upon the number of categories and types of subcategories in your system, select a colour for each of the major categories. For instance:

red file folders = Fingertip Files
blue file folders = Business Files
white file folders = Permanent Files
black file folders = Reference Files

Colour makes it easy for you to see at a glance what files are on your desk and makes it quicker for you to put them away.

Annual Routine

Once a year, you should houseclean your files. We call this the annual "purge" of records, but in fact, you may not have much to destroy. Still, you may have information that is now past your need for frequent reference and can now be stored. An annual appraisal and revisiting of decisions about retention will save you lots of hours. You have already determined what to keep and for how long. During an annual purge, it's a simple matter to check the contents of each file folder to ensure that its contents match the guidelines, then move to storage those records that are no longer needed in the office.

Look forward to the annual purge. Wear your old clothes, work through a pizza lunch, then go golfing as soon as you're done. It's that quick!	**Tip: Get into the Spirit!**

Moving on is exactly what the unneeded records should do during this annual purge. Many businesses make use of available space within their premises to store records, but a few words of caution here. Use available space only if the records can be protected from moisture, temperature fluctuations, pests, dirt and other hazards. Be cautious if you are using a garage, a basement or an attic. Also, make sure that you use storage boxes specially designed to hold records. These are reinforced to hold heavy paper, and their uniform size makes them easier to stack. Label the boxes and arrange them for retrieval—after all, you may still need to refer to them once in a while, and your time is too valuable to waste hunting through a disorganized storage space.

Better than setting up storage in your garage or renting a storage locker are the commercial records storage services you may find in your area. Check your telephone directory to locate these companies, found under such headings as "Office Records Stored" or "Storage—Office Records." These companies offer file retrieval and delivery services, and they will dispose of your confidential business records. The fees are modest when you consider how much time and space you will save.

What to do with the records you no longer need? Delete electronic records no longer needed from your computer directories. Erase computer files from disks and immediately reformat them. In a recent news item, recycled computer disks were found for resale with all their original confidential client data intact. As for your paper records, shred them. Shred these records because you have on them valuable business information or personal client data that should be protected. You don't want your company name on the evening news because someone has found sensitive information from your files waiting in the street for garbage pickup. In one major city, the personal medical records of female patients were found stacked and scattered in a lane. Shred expired records or have them confidentially destroyed by a commercial service to protect you and your clients' information. More on privacy in chapter 6.

A final note: always keep a summary list of records you destroy (grouped by subject and year). In some jurisdictions this may in fact be a requirement. But more importantly, this list eliminates a futile hunt for records that aren't there.

Equipment and Supplies

As mentioned at the beginning of chapter 2, the "right" place for records is a two-part problem—the logical and the physical place. We have already discussed the first part of the "right" place—the logical arrangement of records and their relationship to other records. Here we address the second part of the "right" place—the physical place, the equipment, folders, labelling and related matters. We provide some relatively inexpensive methods for file housekeeping and tips for simplifying the process.

The type of physical place you choose, including containers and storage areas, is governed by three factors: the format of your records, the amount of space you have in which to store them and the kind of containers you feel most comfortable using. *Anything* can be used to store records, providing the records are kept clean, are stored in usable condition, and can be retrieved when desired. If you start by thinking about cabinets and storage equipment, you need to take into account the room available to place the equipment and the types of devices for containing and grouping the records (folders, pockets, binders). If you start by thinking about the devices, you need to take into account the form of document or record: is it a paper document or in another medium, such as a computer disk, photograph, engineering drawing or videotape?

Let's begin by looking at the formats your records come in. Quite likely, despite all the computers in use, the bulk of your records are in paper format. Here are options for housing paper documents:

- *file folders*: readily available at most stationery suppliers in standard letter, metric and legal sizes. *Top-tab styles* are designed for file drawers, allowing you to review and read labels across the top edge of the folder, which is presented first when you roll open the drawer. *Side-tab styles* are designed for shelves, allowing you to review and read labels from the side of the folder, which is presented first. Folders are inexpensive, have room for labels, come in a variety of colours (which adapt to a colour-coded system) and can expand to accommodate a growing amount of paper information.

Tip: Pick the Size That Suits

What folder size should you select? Pick the smallest size needed to match your documents. If most of your correspondence is standardized to letter or metric, a larger folder will not be necessary. Fold over the occasional larger documents you may have. Large file folders cost more and take up more of your valuable storage space.

- *pocket file folders*: readily available in several sizes, and designed in a heavier material to hold a larger group of related papers. Pocket files are usually expansive, designed with accordion folding to grow as the volume of paper expands inside. Pocket files may have top or side tabs or may have a complete cover, with rope or elastic to hold the papers in place within the folder. Usually these are more expensive than regular folders, because of their heavier construction. They are ideal for case records and client or project files because they are portable.

- *binders*: ring and clamp-style binders can perform the same function as file folders. They can hold paper records, either by means of holes punched in the papers or by clamps designed to hold papers in place. The binders are sturdily constructed, will protect records and are conveniently portable for taking to job sites, meetings and so on. Top-loading sheet protectors will hold small items and protect valuable papers from marks, moisture and excessive handling.

Now let's look at the furniture or equipment available to house folders or binders:

- *filing cabinets*: available in two styles. Usually constructed of metal, which is strong enough to bear the weight of paper, these styles of cabinets hold folders upright for easy retrieval and refiling. Often these can be locked, to provide extra security for records. *Drawer-style cabinets* have two to five drawers, which roll out when you are accessing files. When planning your office layout, you have to remember to leave room for the rollout. *Shelf-style cabinets* have two to six or seven shelves, which are fixed and don't move. The cover door will flip up when open, and you see the files from the side view. This latter style takes up less floor space, because you don't have to leave room for the rolling drawer. These are also taller, with more shelves, because without pullout shelves, they do not overbalance.
- *fireproof cabinets*: very heavy (watch the floor loading here) and usually about five times the cost of conventional metal cabinets. These will have some sort of underwriters' fire rating (two hours, three hours, etc.) that indicates the length of time the contents will withstand

hot temperatures of a particular range. These are designed to hold paper or other document formats. Normally you would only consider a fireproof cabinet for records if they were vital to the operation of your business.

Each style of filing cabinet and fireproof cabinet will hold folders, pockets or binders, if the drawers or shelves are deep enough. Some types of cabinets are modular, meaning that drawers or shelves can be replaced to hold storage units for computer disks, videotapes or information in other formats.

If space is limited, consider other less conventional containers. Look in home furniture stores or lifestyle shops to find different types of containers suitable for your records. Consider containers constructed from wicker, cardboard or other materials. These are portable and stackable if your office space is tight and you need to put your records away.

Tip: Order by Phone or On-Line If You Can

Shop from the comfort of your office. Use Internet sites or the toll-free telephone lines often listed in suppliers' catalogues to order supplies, even from local vendors. Sometimes delivery is free with a modest minimum order. Your time is money—take advantage of any such services where they are available.

Boxing and Storing Inactive Records

We have already discussed the principle that once you are finished using records, you should remove them from your office area and move them to storage. We want to briefly discuss this process, called *file transfer,* from the perspective of equipment and storage space.

When you no longer refer to the records, it makes sound economic sense to pack them up (we're referring to paper records here) into storage boxes and get the boxes out of your office space. You then have room for more current information in your office, and you don't waste time or money storing information you don't need to have on hand.

First, let's examine the container. Tote boxes are made from cardboard specifically designed to hold paper records, and they are much less expensive than conventional filing cabinets. We recommend that you spend the money to buy the correct containers rather than be thrifty and try to recycle cardboard boxes. Paper is heavy, and regular boxes are constructed with glue. As time passes, the glue will dry and your recycled box will fall apart. There is nothing more devastating than picking up a stored box of records and having the bottom give way, scattering your records all over.

Make a list of the contents in your boxes of stored records. Keep one copy in your files for reference, so that you can retrieve records from storage. Place one copy in the box, to act as an inventory of the box.

The other aspect of managing inactive records is where you place the boxed records. If you have access to a commercial-records storage service, we strongly urge you to use the service, rather than try to set up your own storage area. Commercial firms offer a safe, secure, clean storage facility, with full retrieval service if you need to get your records back. When the records are no longer needed, these facilities will also provide records destruction.

6
Security and Privacy

FROM THE NEWS HEADLINES:

- "Women's medical records strewn on lawn"
- "Second stack of insurance papers found not shredded"
- "Restaurant fire destroys office, records"
- "Fire destroys records at insurance company"
- "Bungled beach bonfire of medical files fuels ire"
- "Private medical records flood Kingston man's fax machine: Repeated complaints failed to stop flow of psychiatric reports"
- "Flaw in e-mail security makes a potential hole for hackers"

This sampling of newspaper headlines provides some thought-provoking examples of misfortune and the mismanagement of business information. Ask yourself: "If a fire struck my business tonight, would I be able to resume operation tomorrow? If a thief stole my computer, would I know who owed me money and what orders I have to process? Am I really protecting the privacy of my clients or customers from accidental disclosure? Is my business at risk of bad publicity from careless disclosure procedures?"

We have previously discussed the value of records to your organization and have discussed why you are keeping records. In this chapter we review your business records from the perspective of protection and security, to enable you to evaluate which records are vital to the survival of your company. This discussion is about protecting the physical properties and content of records. Although you likely carry insurance to protect aspects of your business, records are generally not appraised or insured, yet the value of the information contained in records is incalculable. And, increasingly, the need to keep information secure from unauthorized users is, if not an obligation, an expectation of business owners.

Protecting Your Records

We have already discussed the fact that some of your records are essential for the protection of your business operation. We call these vital or critical records, and they are the keys to maintaining or resuming your business should you suffer a disaster—a fire, a flood, a storm or a theft of your office equipment. A sad statistic: 80 percent of all small businesses struck by a fire or other disaster don't resume operation afterwards. Part of the failure is attributed to the inability of business owners to re-establish processes after the disaster is over.

Although there are many factors affecting postdisaster business resumption, access to and use of business records is crucial. Consider your records from the perspective of what is necessary for the re-establishment of the business and the seamless resumption of operation.

First, you need to decide what disasters you should worry about. Do you live in an area that is subject to sudden storms? Are you in a region vulnerable to earthquakes? If a sudden, unplanned event (like a tornado or earthquake) would create havoc for your business, then those are the disasters you should plan for and protect your business against. The most probable disaster in any region is fire. Industry statistics indicate that fire is the most likely disaster to affect a business. Your insurance coverage will likely protect your premises and equipment, so we will assume you have that part of your business planning already taken care of. What we want you to ask yourself is "What are the records I need to carry on with my business, and where are they?"

Identification of these records should be a factor in your decision-making around "how long to keep and why," the retention guidelines discussed in chapter 3. Keep in mind that vital records will probably form only about 5 percent of your total collection of records. Unlike your permanent records, however, these records may only be vital until a business cycle is complete, for example, until an invoice is paid.

Consider this five-step strategy for identifying and dealing with vital records:

1. Identify vital records when appraising your information and highlight them on your file list. (Label them "critical records" or "vital records" or use a "red dot" sticker on the file folders.)
2. Train all staff to understand the importance of these records.
3. Determine for how long they are vital (for example, until bill is paid, until loan is repaid, until the company year-end is completed).
4. Find a simple way to protect them (see next section).
5. Review the status of these records during your monthly and annual file maintenance routines.

Protecting Your Vital Records

Usually the simplest way to protect any records that you need to keep is to store them in a separate location. Disasters usually deprive you of access to your business premises. You might need to be able to operate your business, for a time, in a separate location. A duplicate set of records means you can get right back to business quickly, even before you reoccupy your office. Unless a disaster is widespread, it is unlikely that two premises will be struck by the same disaster at the same time, so your duplicate set of records should be available for use. (If widespread disaster is a real possibility, look farther afield for a safe place to store your critical records!)

As we have discussed, the best way to protect vital records is to keep the original documents in a safe and remote location such as a bank vault and use a duplicate copy in your office for working purposes. For your computer files, creating a copy and placing the copy off-site is the simplest way to avoid loss.

As you evaluate your records, you may discover that they are already protected because they are duplicated as part of the business cycle. For example, your accountant may have a copy of your invoices. Where this "natural" duplication exists, you do not need to do anything other than identify the location of the duplicate records.

The easiest way to protect your vital records is to perform the duplication, or movement off-site, during a logical phase of the business cycle. For instance, if it is your accounts receivable records you need to worry about, then create a duplicate of your invoices on a backup computer disk when you prepare the outgoing invoices. Take the backup disk off-site. Replace it when you prepare the next set of bills.

Protecting your records is not as much work as it sounds. There are only a few records you need to worry about, and it is usually a simple matter to introduce a duplication process into your routine. Consider this extra care of your records a form of insurance. You will not know how valuable the process is until you have to use it.

Privacy of Records

Your records are important business tools. Strictly from a security perspective, you will want to ensure their protection. But you may also need to ensure the privacy of your records. You may have records that include *personal information* about people.

Personal information is anything that is a personal identifier—information that describes someone or can be attributed to someone—*regardless of who created the information*. Obvious personal information is an individual's name, address, telephone number and social insurance, social security or national insurance number. Other personal identifiers include religious beliefs, health information, physical characteristics, political affiliations and so on. The key concept here is that it doesn't matter whether your company created the information; if it is about someone, then it is considered his or her personal information.

There is increasing concern about the protection of personal privacy in many jurisdictions. Within a number of countries, there are legislated requirements for protecting the privacy of personal records. Regulations aside, however, maintaining privacy of records makes good business sense. Which would you rather deal with—a business that leaves your personal information out in the garbage for the world to discover or a business that uses, stores and disposes of your personal information in a confidential manner? Adopt for your business the standards you would like other businesses to follow in handling *your* personal information.

The concern about privacy grows as the creation, distribution and storage of business information increasingly becomes computer based. Fear of unauthorized disclosure or access to personal information causes people to distrust agencies that collect and use personal data. If your business collects or uses personal information, part of your research into regulations that affect your business should be a review of your obligations with regards to personal information.

Here are some general guidelines to help you, even if you are not bound by any regulations or codes of practice. These guidelines reflect the principles of fair information practice and are the basis for codes of conduct in organizations that deal with large amounts of personal information. Depending upon the sector in which your business operates, you may be familiar with these and may be voluntarily or by regulation obliged to follow them.

- Let people know in advance that you are collecting their personal information, and let them know the purpose for which you are collecting it.
- If possible, obtain their permission to use personal information or allow them to opt out of providing the information to you.
- Limit the collection of personal data to essential information only. Only collect information that is necessary. Ensure that what is collected is accurate.
- Don't pass on personal information; do not disclose it to any unauthorized agency or company.

- Don't hang on to personal information. Set a retention period and destroy the personal information according to your guidelines.
- Protect the information. Use locked filing cabinets and restrict the number of people with access to the information to those who "need to know" rather than those who would "like to know."
- Permit individuals from whom you have collected information to see it and verify its accuracy.
- Provide a method for individuals to seek redress about their information.

These guidelines are based upon a document developed by the Organization for Economic Co-operation and Development (OECD), *Guidelines on the Protection of Privacy and Transborder Flows of Personal Data*. Refer to Appendix B for other sources on personal-information practices.

While you may not have to follow these guidelines by law or by agreement, they are the basis for legislation and codes of professional practice in many jurisdictions and business sectors. Why not try to put your practices in line with all these other groups? A good rule of thumb worth repeating: Treat the personal information of others the way you would like to see others care for your own personal information.

7
Under Control
Dealing with Growth and Change

BY NOW, YOU SHOULD BE FEELING PRETTY PROUD OF YOURSELF, because you have laid the foundation for ongoing control over your business information. You now have a method for receiving, organizing, using and finally protecting or disposing of your business records. You should not experience any difficulties in finding and using information. And certainly you will have no more indecision about what information to keep and what to get rid of. Well done!

However, your record-keeping system is never finished. The volume and type of information will also be a reflection of the activities in your business. As your business grows and you add new functions in your organization, your information will expand and diversify in its subjects and functions. If you add or change the technologies in your organization, the changes may affect the records generated. External regulations may also change, necessitating changes to records and information systems. Consequently, you will need to regularly review your record-keeping system to ensure that the procedures, classification system and retention schedules still meet the needs of your business.

We have already encouraged you to periodically review your information management practices. This review should be conducted in order to ensure the adequacy of all aspects of the processes you have established. To ensure that you have established the required controls over the various information resources in your office, review the following questions. If you can answer yes to the questions, you can be confident that you have control of your information.

An Office Record-Keeping Checklist

Management of current information:

- Do you have processes in place to handle the current information received or generated in the business?
- Do you have a file plan that works for records in all formats, including computer directories?
- Is your filing system adequate to handle the information needed for the daily operation of the business?
- Do you have a place to maintain the information and records you need for the daily operation of the business?
- Do you know when you no longer need to keep information for daily use?
- Do you have a storage location for your inactive information?

How long to keep information:

- Do you know what the legal requirements are for keeping information?
- In addition to legal requirements, do you know how long you have to keep information?
- Have you identified the required time for keeping your records? Is this time period recorded on the file plan?

Protection of information:

- Do you have a backup process for ensuring your electronic records are protected?

- Do you know what the vital records are for your company?
- Do you know where the vital records are located?
- Do you have protective measures in place to ensure vital records survive any disasters that occur?
- Do you have the permanent records of your company in safekeeping?
- Do you protect the privacy of personal information in your records?

Disposal of information:

- Do you know what information you can destroy?
- Do you have confidential destruction procedures in place?
- Do you keep a list of destroyed records?

Documentation and training:

- Have you prepared written procedures for managing your company records?
- Have you prepared a routine timetable for records review, transfer and disposal?
- Do you train staff to be familiar with and follow these procedures?

Final Words

What to keep? Where to put it? For how long? Why? Are my records secure? We hope this book has provided you with the information you need to make informed decisions about the setup, management and care of your business information.

Although you'll never be done—managing information is a continuous process—once you've taken the time to set up your files, caring for your information on a routine basis should take relatively little of your limited time. Effectively organizing and managing your business information is a key toward business success.

By now, you are well on your way to saving money, time and your corporate memory by implementing the suggestions we have provided in the preceding chapters. We have taken the principles of information management as practised by big organizations and distilled them into commonsense procedures for the smallest of organizations. If you implement these suggestions, you will have confident answers to the questions of what to keep? Where to put it? For how long and why? You will know your records are secure, and all your business information will be at your fingertips in the office!

Appendix A: Hands On

THE SYSTEM OUTLINED IN THIS BOOK DIVIDES PAPER FILES INTO four broad categories: Fingertip, Business, Permanent and Reference Files. There are many ways to set up these files—and certainly all of these categories could be contained in file folders in a filing cabinet. However, we suggest incorporating the Fingertip Files into a binder, with the remaining files being kept in the more conventional file folder setup.

Whether you use file folders, binders or any other container, make the look and feel of your company files suit the aesthetic and functional preference of you or your office staff. In this section you will find hands-on, step-by-step instructions for setting up and accessing your Fingertip Files using a binder system, divided into the three subcategories of *Calendar, Contacts/Organizations* and *Receipts*, followed by some examples of how to use the binder. Further hands-on instructions are provided for setting up the remaining files—Business, Permanent and Reference—using both paper and electronic file folders.

As with any task, it might help to break down this one into manageable pieces. We suggest you set aside one afternoon to read through these instructions and gather together your supplies, then spend the following afternoon putting together your Fingertip Files binder and conventional files.

Setting Up Fingertip Files

A binder keeps all your Fingertip Files information together in one portable container. It's easy to grab your binder as you head off to visit a client or job site, and it's comforting to know your schedule and contact information is all in one place.

You will need the following supplies to set up your Fingertip Files binder:

- a one-inch or one-and-a-half-inch binder with a clear spine label. Look for one that also has a handy pocket on the inside front and inside back cover.
- extra-wide tab dividers
- a current 12-month calendar (three-hole punched)
- clear-plastic business card holder sheets for three-ring binders
- 36 heavy-duty, top-loading sheet protectors (add more as necessary)
- 33 sheets of 8½-by-11-inch sheets of paper (add more as necessary)

The number of dividers, business card holders and sheet protectors you need will depend on the volume of information you need to keep at your fingertips.

Assembly

1. Label your binder with the name of your business. Include a telephone number in case the binder gets misplaced.
2. Label the tab dividers as follows: "Calendar," "Monthly Info," "Daily Info," "Contact/Organizations" and "Receipts." (If necessary, label the remaining tab dividers with categories of information you decide should also be kept

here, such as "Automobile—Mileage," if you will be taking the binder with you when you leave the office on business.) Place dividers in the binder.

Calendar Section

3. Insert a current 12-month calendar behind the tab divider labelled "Calendar."
4. Insert 12 sheet protectors behind the tab divider labelled "Monthly Info."
5. Take 12 of the 8½-by-11-inch sheets of paper and label them by month (one month for each sheet of paper—"January," "February," and so on). Place the sheet marked "January" into the first sheet protector behind "Monthly Info." Place the remaining months in date order into the sheet protectors that follow.
6. Insert 16 sheet protectors behind the tab divider labelled "Daily Info."
7. Take 16 of the remaining 8½-by-11-inch sheets of paper. On the first sheet write "Day 1." On the reverse side of the sheet, write "Day 2." On the next sheet write "Day 3" on the front, "Day 4" on the reverse and so on, until "Day 31." (Note: there will be no writing on the reverse side of the Day 31 sheet.) Place the sheets into the sheet protectors behind "Daily Info."

Contacts/Organizations Section

8. Place several of the business card holder sheets designed for three-ring binders behind the tab divider labelled "Contacts/Organizations."
9. Take one 8½-by-11-inch sheet of paper. Write "New Numbers/Addresses" on the sheet and place it into a sheet protector. Place it in the binder behind the business card holders.

10. After "New Numbers/Addresses," place as many sheet protectors as necessary to hold any schedules or contact lists you want to keep handy.

Receipts Section

11. Place at least four sheet protectors behind the tab divider labelled "Receipts."
12. Take at least four 8½-by-11-inch sheets of paper. Write on them categories such as "Banking Receipts," "Credit Card Receipts," "Expense Receipts," "Expense Receipts—Project A" or "Coupons and Offers." Create as many categories as necessary to keep track of your financial information and transaction receipts.

How to Use the Fingertip Binder

Use the monthly "Calendar" section to jot down appointments, callback reminders and bills to pay. Use the sheet protectors (referred to as pockets from now on) to hold any information, notes or documents, such as invitations or airline tickets, that you might need on a particular day or during a particular month. Use the "Daily Info" pockets labelled "Day 1" through "Day 31" to keep track of information needed during the current month. The "Monthly Info" pockets are used to store information needed in the future, for the following month and beyond. At the end of the current month, we'll call it January, all the daily pockets should be empty (because you've already used the information). Take the documents out of the following monthly pocket, in this example February, and place them into the appropriate daily pockets under "Daily Info."

The business card holders in the *Contacts/Organizations* section give you easy access to your collection of business cards, while the clear pockets keep information about organizations and associated calendars of events, as well as transportation schedules (bus, train), handy. Alternatively, you might choose to three-hole punch your papers and place them directly into the binder. However, you'll still find some pockets useful to store odd-sized papers or folded brochures.

Use the pockets in the *Receipts* section to keep together in one temporary convenient spot all your receipts from financial transactions—everything from banking receipts to credit card purchase receipts to parking receipts. Understand that this is a temporary holding spot until information can be verified against statements or re-distributed into the Business Files.

The Fingertip Binder in Action—An Example

It's been another busy January day . . .

Up at the crack of dawn, you head off to the local business club breakfast meeting and connect with a number of interesting contacts, securing three business cards. Things are definitely looking up: A.J., a much-sought-after contact, hands you a scrap of paper with the coveted cellphone number written on it. The club organizers have prepared a handout listing all the events and activities scheduled for the upcoming year. Next stop the bank machine, to deposit that long-awaited cheque that arrived late yesterday afternoon by courier. Since you have been surviving on coins only lately, this seems like an opportune time to withdraw some cash to tide you over for a while. You walk past a community kiosk and notice the new commuter train schedule is there. You don't use it that often, but it's handy to have a copy in the office, so you grab one. A quick glance at your watch and you decide to turn in to the stationery store. A routine stop for supplies adds $75 to your credit card and an electronic organizer to your wish list. Oops—no time to spare now, but the glare of the gas light on your car's dashboard convinces you, short of time or not, you must stop for fuel. A partial fill and $15 later you're on your way again. By now there's no time to look for free street parking, so you head directly to the pay parking lot. Your client meeting goes remarkably well, and you promise to phone them back on the 19th. Even the $7.50 parking tab can't dampen your spirits now.

Back at the office, a slim but promising assortment of mail awaits your attention. It includes an invitation to a product presentation (including a free lunch) next month, a couple of bills to pay, a note from the real estate agent who just sold the property next door, and your airline tickets for your business but mostly pleasure trip to New York City. You're anxious to get on with that proposal for this morning's client, but you know that if you want to keep your papers and information under control, you need to empty the receipts and business cards from your briefcase and sort the mail.

You decide to start with the mail. You want that free lunch next month, besides, it does look like a useful presentation. Where does the invite go? Open your Fingertip Binder to the first section—the "Calendar" section. Mark the date on your calendar, then file the invitation under "Monthly Info" in the pocket labelled "February." You routinely pay your bills on the 15th and 30th. Since it's past the 15th, put the bills in the "Daily Info" pocket marked "Day 30." Mark bills to pay on the calendar if you want, however, a routine check of the daily pockets will remind you to pay them. Once they are paid, transfer the bill statements into the Business Files. Toss the note from the real estate agent, because you're not thinking about a property move at this time or in the near future. Besides, if you do move, you'll enlist the help of your relative the real estate agent, rather than cause a family feud. The tickets to New York get filed in the "Daily Info" pocket marked "Day 21." The trip has already been pencilled in on the calendar.

Now on to the briefcase. After the meeting today, you need to call the client back on the 19th, so write yourself a summary note and place it in the daily pocket marked "Day 19." You'll see it when you check the contents of the pocket before you "close up shop" the night before or first thing in the morning.

You have three new business cards from the breakfast meeting. Right now there's no action required, but you'd like to keep the cards for future reference. Place them into the business card holders in the *Contacts/Organizations* section of your binder. The scrap of paper from A.J. with the cellphone number on it goes into the pocket marked "New Numbers/Addresses" until you have time to update your phone list. You glance at the handout of business club events and activities. Nothing pressing pops out at the moment, but you'll want to refer to the handout over the course of the year, so you decide to file it in a pocket within the *Contacts/Organizations* section. While you're there, turn to the pocket with schedules in it. Toss out the old commuter train schedule and replace it with the new one you've picked up.

Flip over to the *Receipts* section. Put the transaction receipts for both the deposit and the cash withdrawal into the pocket labelled "Banking Receipts." Keep them there until you can verify these transactions against a forthcoming statement issued by your financial institution. Once the statement is verified, shred the transaction receipts.

Then there's the $75 credit card receipt, $20 cash gas receipt and the $7.50 parking receipt. File the office supplies receipt in the "Credit Card Receipts" pocket. After you've verified it against the statement you will transfer it to the appropriate expense folder in the Business Files. The cash gas and parking receipts go into the "Expense Receipts" pocket, until you have time to record these expenses and sort the receipts into the appropriate expense folders in the Business Files.

Timewise, you've spent only a few minutes sorting the information, but you've saved yourself precious time finding it again in the future. Now, with your papers and information under control, it's back to business . . .

Setting Up Business, Permanent and Reference Files

As with the Fingertip Files, you may choose to use a binder system rather than file folders for the paper records in your Business, Permanent and Reference Files. However, because this is where the greatest volume of your records will be found, we expect that file folders and labels will be more practical for housing your records.

You will need to buy some file folders, probably letter-size, in a top-tab style for drawer storage or in a side-tab style for storage on a shelf. You will also want to have labels on which to type or write your file names. If you selected categories from the Filing System at a Glance (pages 36 to 39), you will need approximately 60 folders, although you will need more if you use one file folder per customer. If you want to use distinctive colours to represent each category, then the breakdown is approximately 35 for the Business Files, 10 for the Permanent Files and 15 for the Reference Files. Remember, you can also introduce colours by choosing colour-coded labels.

Assembly

1. From the list of file subjects in this book, select the subjects that describe your files. See pages 36 to 39 for a list of suggested subjects using either alphabetic descriptors or numeric codes and chapter 3 for further breakdowns. Mark your selected subjects with a highlighter pen right in this book, pencilling in new subjects, or make your own separate list.
2. Prepare a file folder for each subject required and label each folder on its tab. If you are coding your files, place the coding and the subject or title on the file folder. It's also important to put the date you open or create the file folder, so that you can later easily identify the date range of the records in your file. This will help you move the records on to storage when they are no longer required.
3. Sort your Business, Permanent and Reference Files into the selected subjects as you go through them. (If you have a lot of papers to sort through and organize, you should write the code or subject in pencil on each document to be filed.)
4. File the documents into the file folders, placing them in date order (oldest documents at the back, most recent document in front).

5. Arrange the folders in alphabetical or numeric order and put them into the drawer, box or container (or onto the shelf) you've selected as a home for these records.

How to Use the Business, Permanent and Reference Files

On a regular basis, add information from the Fingertip Files and incoming mail into the Business or Reference Files. On a monthly basis, review your system, adjusting and creating new categories as needed. On an annual basis, move records into the Permanent Files, remove unneeded records for disposal, and move records from active office space to storage.

Setting Up Electronic Files

Follow the same system for organizing your electronic records as you have established for your information in paper format. Here is a model for setting up your Business, Permanent and Reference Files on a stand-alone personal computer.

The operating system for the model is Microsoft Windows 95, and the framework is the tree structure established within the Windows Explorer setup. (A "tree" is an apt description for this setup, as it follows a broad to more specific hierarchy, just as a tree has a trunk with larger branches leading to smaller branches and leaves.)

Establish a top-level folder called "My Business," which will provide the home for your records, no matter where they are created in your operating system (for example, in MS Word, MS Excel, Access, Powerpoint). Having a single home for your records facilitates computer backup procedures, because all of your computer records can be found within this one "branch" of your tree.

Within "My Business," create a folder for each of the three categories—Business, Permanent and Reference. To store inactive records, create another folder called "Storage."

With your list of selected file topics beside you, take the Business Files folder and, within it, create a folder for each of the following if they apply to your business needs: Administration; Equipment, Supplies and Services; Finance; Personnel and Staffing; Premises; and Operations. Then, depending upon how much information you anticipate creating or receiving, establish the appropriate subjects or topics within these categories. For example, if you have few employees, require little in the way of supplies, and have a single leased premise, you may not need to further subdivide your categories. As you create documents on your computer, save them under these categories. On the other hand, if you have lots of clients, then under the Operations category, you will create individual folders for each client.

On a regular basis, review your files and remove documents to the "Storage" folder if they are not active. Review your file structure and make adjustments as needed.

Be sure to move your electronic-mail messages to these categories if they relate to your business, or create a similar structure if your operating system will not permit you to file e-mail with your internally generated files.

Directory of Business Records

Here's an example of how a list (or directory) of folders might appear:

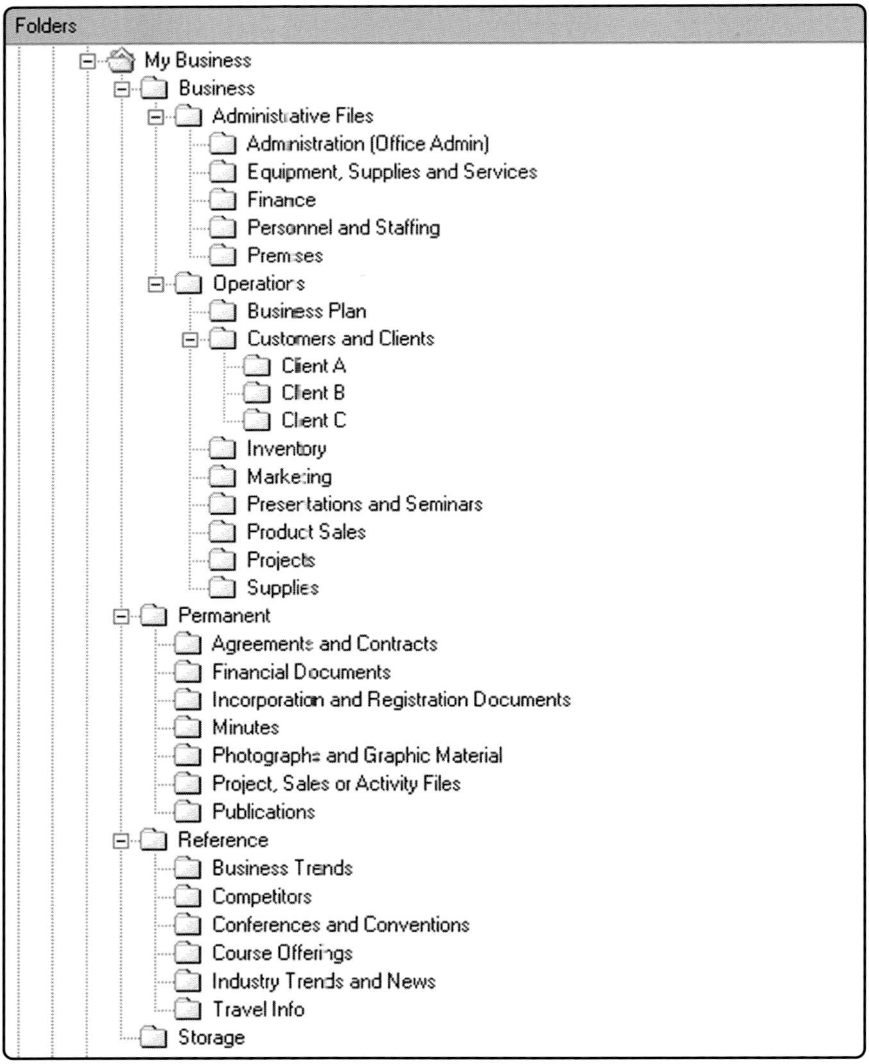

Appendix B: Resources

Learning More about Information Management

HERE IS SOME INFORMATION TO HELP YOU, THE SMALL-BUSINESS owner, in your search for resources or specific information related to aspects of your record-keeping needs. These resources include: taxation authorities; government information; services to small business; professional associations and organizations; office suppliers and outfitters; books on office management for the small business; and books on records and information management.

Websites

The World Wide Web provides an extensive source of information, including contacts for taxation authorities and government agencies, professional associations and business support bodies. Most of these websites include electronic forms, as well as practical and clear instructions, with particular emphasis on the needs of small business. Of benefit are the following:

Taxation Authorities

Government taxation authorities around the world have posted information to assist business organizations with the records associated with taxation. Examples include:

Australia. Australian Tax Office
www.ato.gov.au
Includes instructions for small business, including directions for keeping records.

Canada. Canada Customs and Revenue Agency
www.ccra-adrc.gc.ca

New Zealand. Inland Revenue Department
www.ird.govt.nz

United Kingdom. Inland Revenue
www.inlandrevenue.gov.uk
Includes information for self-assessment, leading to specific information on what records to keep.

United States of America. Internal Revenue Service
www.irs.gov/bus_info
Includes helpful links for the small-business owner.

Tip: Start at Home	Don't get distracted in cyberspace. Search for your own government website first. It will always have links to other related and relevant sites.

Government Information

Each of these specific sites includes current policies on government records practices, lists of holdings, links to key sites and other valuable information for researchers. Examples include:

National Archives of Australia
www.naa.gov.au
Contains policy information on records management (including links to the Australian Standard for Records Management—AS 4390), electronic records management, records as evidence and related information.

National Archives of Canada
www.archives.ca
Contains federal-government policy information, including nine publications relating to managing electronic records in an electronic work environment.

United States National Archives and Records Administration
www.nara.gov

United Kingdom
The National Archives Public Record Office
www.pro.gov.uk/recordsmanagement

Services to Small Business

British Columbia Business Service Centre
www.sb.gov.bc.ca

Canadian Women's Business Network
www.cdnbizwomen.com

National Association for the Self-Employed
www.nase.org

National Federation of Independent Businesses
www.nfibonline.com

Professional Associations and Organizations

Professional associations focus on specific aspects of information management. These organizations produce technical bulletins, conference proceedings and publications. Here are the names of some to consider contacting for information.

Association of Canadian Archivists
P.O. Box 2596, Station D
Ottawa, ON K1P 5W6
http://aca.archives.ca

Association for Information and Image Management (AIIM)
1100 Wayne Avenue
Silver Springs, MD 20910-5603
www.aiim.org

ARMA International
4200 Somerset Drive, Suite 215
Prairie Village, KS 66208
(913) 341-3808 or (800) 422-2762 (Canada and U.S.)
www.arma.org
ARMA International is the best North American source for records management information. The association produces a wide range of technical publications and audiovisual materials related to information and records management. Key subjects are filing standards, electronic records management, disaster planning and recovery, records retention guidelines, and use of micrographics and image technology. Its website has links to various affiliated chapters and provides information on events, annual conferences and its on-line bookstore.

Titles published by ARMA include:

Alphabetic Filing Rules (1995). 2nd ed. ISBN 0-933887-58-2

Emergency Management for Records and Information Management Programs (1997), by Virginia A. Jones and Kris E. Keys. ISBN 0-933887-70-1

Software Directory for Records Management Systems (1999), by John Phillips. ISBN 0-933887-84-1

Business Forms Management Association
319 S.W. Third Avenue, Suite 710
Portland, OR 97204-2618
www.teleport.com/~bfma/

International Council on Archives (ICA)
60, rue des Francs-Bourgeois
75003 Paris, France
www.ica.org

International Records Management Trust
12 John Street
London, England WC1N 2EB
www.irmt.org

National Association of Professional Organizers (NAPO)
P.O. Box 140647
Austin, TX 78714
www.napo.net

Records Management Association of Australia
www.taunet.net.au/rmaa/default.html

Records Management Society of Great Britain
Woodside, Coleheath Bottom, Speen
Princes Risborough
Buckinghamshire, England HP27-OSZ
www.rms-gb.org.uk/

Society of American Archivists (SAA)
527 South Wells Street, 5th Floor
Chicago, IL 60607-3922
www.archivists.org

Office Suppliers and Outfitters

Check in your local telephone directory for office suppliers, stationery stores or lifestyle stores in your area where you can obtain the records storage equipment, devices and supplies described in this book. There are many unique and specialized stores. You may already have a favourite. If not, any of the following organizations (many have websites) may be nearby.

Container Store (U.S.)
Hold Everything (U.S.)
The Holding Company (U.K.)
IKEA (worldwide)
Office Depot (Canada and U.S.)
Staples/Business Depot (Canada and U.S.)

Books on Office Management for the Small Business

The following titles are books on general office management subjects specifically oriented to small businesses. You might consult them for further information or an in-depth discussion of subjects we have mentioned in passing.

Eisenberg, Ronni, and Kate Kelly (2000). *Organize Your Home Office! Simple Routines for Setting up an Office at Home.* ISBN 0-7868-8465-7

Pollar, Odette (1999). *Organizing Your Work Space: A Guide to Personal Productivity.* Rev. ed. ISBN 1-56052-522-3

Rosenbaum, Alvin (1995). *The Complete Home Office: Planning Your Work Space for Maximum Efficiency.* ISBN 0-670-85293-7

Treacy, Declan. *Clear Your Desk!* (1998). ISBN 0-09-927192-3

———. *Conquer the Information Mountain* (1998). ISBN 0-09-927095-1

Books on Records and Information Management

Canadian Standards Association. *CAN/CSA-Q830 A Model Code for the Protection of Personal Information*. Canadian Standards Association, 178 Rexdale Boulevard, Etobicoke, ON M9W 1R3. ISSN 0317-5669

Diamond, Suzanne K. (1995). *Records Management: A Practical Guide*. 3rd ed. ISBN 0-8144-0295-X

Organization for Economic Co-operation and Development (OECD). *Guidelines on the Protection of Privacy and Transborder Flows of Personal Data.* Abridged version available at www.oecd.org/dsti/sti/it/secur/prod/PRIV-En.HTM#3

McKinnon, Gordon P., ed. (1986). *Fire Protection Handbook.* 16th ed. Boston, MA: National Fire Protection Association.

Penn, Ira, et al. (1994). *Records Management Handbook.* 2nd ed. ISBN 0-566-07510-6

Ricks, Betty, et al. (1997). *Information and Image Management: A Records Systems Approach.* ISBN 0-17-604252-0

Robek, Mary F., Gerald F. Brown, and David O. Stephens (1995). *Information and Records Management.* 4th ed. ISBN 0-02-801793-5

Acknowledgements

From Sandie

This second Streamline Books publication is inspired by all the clients over the years who have allowed me to discover, by looking at all their complex record-keeping problems, that what they really needed were simple, straightforward solutions.

When one of our mentors congratulated us on publishing our first book, he said, "You have completed the easy part—now you have to sell it!" During the past year, we've had our baptism in the book trade, and his words ring ever true. And so, as we complete our second collaboration, we thank the booksellers who've supported us and helped us to find our market.

I would also like to thank my supportive family, who cheerfully help with displays, promote our book talks, make deliveries and tolerate the endless disruptions to family life. And for her unflagging optimism, energy and vision, I salute Denise.

From Denise

Behind every book there are a myriad of stories. I know that Sandie and I for years to come will cherish, laugh about and shake our heads in disbelief over the funny tales and characters associated with this book—from the newspaper photographer who insisted it was more fun to have workshop delegates throw paper at us than capture our beautifully organized filing systems to a manuscript that disappeared behind the "dark side of the moon," so to speak, as it left the editors' offices in Vancouver, headed to Horsefly, B.C., and finally turned up in England!

For the most part, the players behind the scenes remain the ones involved in our first book, *At Your Fingertips! A Household Filing System That Works for You.* As before, the love and support of friends and family is truly a blessing—my husband, Don, and children Aaron, Wesley, and Diana, to name just a few. It is a pleasure to work with Rick Carty of Carty Design, our editors Naomi Pauls and newly transplanted London resident Theresa Best of Paper Trail Publishing, Jorge Rocha at Friesens (some day we will meet!) and Jeff Bellenie, with our distributor Raincoast Book*Express.* Of course, without Sandie there would be no book.

Index